POETIC VOYAGES WOKING

Edited by Simon Harwin

First published in Great Britain in 2001 by
YOUNG WRITERS
Remus House,
Coltsfoot Drive,
Peterborough, PE2 9JX
Telephone (01733) 890066

All Rights Reserved

Copyright Contributors 2001

HB ISBN 0 75433 260 8
SB ISBN 0 75433 261 6

FOREWORD

Young Writers was established in 1991 with the aim to promote creative writing in children, to make reading and writing poetry fun.

This year once again, proved to be a tremendous success with over 88,000 entries received nationwide.

The Poetic Voyages competition has shown us the high standard of work and effort that children are capable of today. It is a reflection of the teaching skills in schools, the enthusiasm and creativity they have injected into their pupils shines clearly within this anthology.

The task of selecting poems was therefore a difficult one but nevertheless, an enjoyable experience. We hope you are as pleased with the final selection in *Poetic Voyages Woking* as we are.

CONTENTS

Brookwood Primary School
Rosie Partington	1
Katie Edmundson	1
Natalie Craven	2
Kevin Gater	2
Natalie Luke	3
John Lugton	3
Amy Lorman-Parker	4
Fiona Thornton	4
Louisa Mousley	5
Sophie Hobbs	6
Sophie Gilby	7
Robert Devine	7
Bethany Goodway	8

Goldsworth Primary School
Adam Stovold	9
Henry Stanley	10
Gareth Musgrove	11
Rosie Kingston	11
Tanya Lattul	12
Stephanie Evans	12
Sophie Etter	13
Nashmia Zubair	13
Beth McCready	14
Aleesha Sharma	14
William Phelan	15
Rebecca Carter	15
Amy Kingston	16
Stewart Lifton	16
Komil Sarwar	17
Luke Butcher	17
Richard Tervet	18
Hector Stanley	18
Simon Brown	19
Kirstin Hay	19

Hannah Davidson	20
Leah Bray	20
Amelia Skerritt	21
Alex Follett	21
Henna Irshad	22
Samman Nawaz	22
Emma Rashbrook	23
Marco Cala	23
Madeleine King	24
Mark Flewitt	24
Ben Matthews	25
Joe Ensoll	25
Ellie Davey	26
Stephanie Holden	26
Holly Taylor	27
Christopher Lodge	27
Craig Ellis	28
Meriam Ahmed	29
Eleanor Wilmott	30
Joseph Grilli	30
Emma Riddell	31
Charlotte Oswick	31
Annabel McKnespiey	32
Amber Lay	32
Jennifer Clarke	33
Tanya Advani	34
Claire Bowerman	35
Lianne Saunders	36
Jonathan Boxall	36
Shehryar Sarwar	37
Alex Paterson	38
Daniel Barbato	39
Rebecca Evans	39
Louise Cook	40
Rebecca Sullivan	40
Elizabeth Turnbull	41
Lucy Lord	41
Sahnya Razaq	42

Laura Holdaway	42
Gemma Tong	43
Rebecca Pateman	43
Rebecca Piggott	44
Alison Sayers	45
Emma Whitehead	46
Gabriel McLoughlin	46
Emma Denty	47
Ben Grilli	47
Daniel Addison	48
Ben Moss	48
Ben Peppitt	49
Sarah Piggott	49
Emma Colbourn	50
Ashwin Sharma	50
Vanessa Baquer	51
Georgina Melville	51
Brendon Sanger	52
Sammy Creasey	52
Rubiya Karim	53
Abigail Lay	53
Adrian Roux	54
Miles Harty	54

Halstead School

Lucy Watson	55
Candice Cocks	55
Natasha Osborne	56
Stephanie Denning	57
Camilla Whittington	58
Charlotte Jackson	59
Charlie Grahame	60
Elizabeth Tweedy	61
Faye Everard	62
Becky Rosenberg	63
Shelley Eastwood	64
Julia Davies	65
Rachel Lovibond	66

Jane Moffat	66
Hazel Williams	67
Martha Williams	68
Francesca Dadlani	68
Laetitia Ward	69
Rosie Burt	69
Joanna Ward	70
Madeleine Dellner	70
Charlotte Worrall	71
Lara Redman	72
Clare Bourke	72
Jessica Elphick	73
Dominique Dron	74
Anna Redbond	75
Jennifer Douglas	76
Lucie Crawford	77
Alice Vassallo	78

St Dunstans RC Primary School

Denise Wakeford	79
Craig Woodhams	80
Rachel Sullivan	80
Chloe Mamet	81
Miranda Smith	82
Daniel Donovan	82
Rachael Jordan	83
Hannah-Jade Murphy	83
Kelly Hockley	84
Felicity Arthur-Worsop	85
David Legrand	86
James Fowkes	86
Natasia Szagun	87
Nicola Pogorzelski	88
Robert McClurey	88
Steven Andrew Nolan	89
Stephanie Colairo	89
Gino Weller	90
Catherine Morrison	90

Jamie Morris	91
Hannah Fidge	92
Craig Cox	92
Theo Jones	93
Jack Bertolone	93
Victoria Valente	94
Kelly Burns	94
Christopher Mulvihill	95
Kate Honeywood	95
Ross Irving	96
Cathryn Samuels	97
Michelle Roche	98

The Hermitage School

Rachel Harrison	98
Chris Parker	99
Christopher Harper	99
Victoria Marshall	100
Mike Slade	100
Clare Hadley	101
Jack Pettifer	102
Hannah Brassil	102
Natasha Blackledge	103
Michael Todd	103
Mark Boylett	104
Jeffrey Rawson	104
Laura Hart	105
Simon Jones	106
John McCormick	106
Claire Couzens	107
Matt Broderick	108
Phoebe Robertson	108
Leanne Harrison	109
Faye Elliott	109
Frances Henderson	110
Scott Gill	110
Thomas Eker	111
Vanessa Ma	111

Lauren Pink	112
Sarah Rhodes-Brown	113
Steven Bartlett	114
Andrew Lawrence	114
Hannah Wood	115
Ryan Meeks	115
Vanessa Reid	116
Poppy Evans	117
Jade Podmore	118
Alix Snell	119
Paul Martin	120
Thomas Smith	120
Eleanor Beamish	121
Michael Veale	121
Stephanie Sale	122
Robert Scott	122
Shakira Westbrooke	123
Briony Chamberlain	123
Sara Dunford	124
Adam Charman	124
James O'Daly	125
Aaron Broderick	125
Mikey Burningham	126
Jack Slater	126
Lisa Russell	127
Lauren Buffone	127
Jessica Lawrence	128
Rachel Thornber	128
Amy Potts	129
Robbie J Ashton	129
Rikkie Letch	130
Robert Estcourt	130
Jack Sollis	131
Yashar Baghri	131
Conor Carr	132
Alana Francis	133
Juliana Mills	133
Lauren Reynolds	134

Jack Warren	134
Becky Partridge	135
Kate Greentree	135
Rebecca Thornber	136
Rachel Tooley	136
Anna O'Dell	137
Daniel Oliver	137
Alexander Ward	138
Emma Wakefield	138
Oliver Grant	139
Daisy Hulke	139
Rosie Hart	140
Lee Massey	140
Emily Lacy	141
Ellie Date	141
Michael Bird	142
Aaron Gauntlett	142
Nathaniel Vries	143
Dani Simancas	144
Laura Quinn	144
Peter John Morgan	145
Ben Lawn	145
Matthew O'Daly	146
Rachel Wheeler	146
Jack Reynolds	147
Leah Bannister	147
Shauna Fox	148
Luke Nye	148
Amy Dillon	149
Ella Walding	149
Catherine Taylor	150
Faye Groves	150
Megan Riley	150
Ellen Potts	151
Hannah James	151
Georgia Smith	151
Dan Hart	152
Katie Mynard	152

Hannah Knox	153
Matthew Beamish	153
Hayley Chappell	154
Luca Naclerio	154
Henry Deacon	155
Daniel Marshall	155
Grace Millican	156
Jade McGill	156
Lotty Eker	157
Alex Davison	158
Bradley McManus	158
Melissa Jones	159
Josh Preece	159
Stephanie Gale	160
Natalie Howard	160
James Gale	161
Jessica Green	161
Laura Atkinson	162
Leila Prescott	162
Rebecca Prior	163
Gemma Collyer	163
Stephanie Snook	164
Julie Roffey	164
Bryony Rose Lambert	165
Stephen Sweetland	166
Jessie Hart	166
Emma Clarke	167
Kellie Le Marquand	168
Jack Eker	168
Rachel Gill	169
Daniel Fisher	170
Lydia Day	170

The Poems

I Should Like To...

I should like to paint the anger of a lion
facing an invader or the passion of a fairy
princess falling at her lover's feet.

I would love to hear the whispers of
forbidden thoughts from someone else's mind.
The silent scream of a flower when it's picked.

I would like to feel the fluffy silver lining
of every cloud in the sky.

I would love to see a fleet of flying white horses
soaring past the moon and to feel their tickly manes.

I would love to paint the happiness of a family
around the Christmas tree on a frosty morning.

Rosie Partington (11)
Brookwood Primary School

My Head

Above my head the sky is rumbling,
Around my head are all the good times I have had,
In front of my head is the life I am waiting for,
Behind my head is all the sadness I have ever known,
Beside my head is my twin who does everything I do,
Inside my head is a sea ever changing.
Far from my head is the fighting and war,
Beneath my head are colours, colours of happiness,
        Colours of sadness,
In the centre of my head my thoughts are swirling,
Outside my head the world is spinning.

Katie Edmundson (11)
Brookwood Primary School

IN MY BAG

In my bag would be . . .

A conker with the skin all cracked.
A pair of socks still neatly packed.
A letter that was never posted.
Some boys kept pet frogs - well most did.
A picture of my mum and dad.
A note to say that I was bad.
An exciting book read through twice.
Some lolly sticks (they were nice!)
A pretty shell from my gran.
A picture of me with a tan.
A purse of money, about three pound.
A torch that was lost but now is found.
An empty carton from the drinks machine.
A mouldy orange now gone green.
My oldest T-shirt, a dirty rag.
That's what would be in my bag.

Natalie Craven (11)
Brookwood Primary School

TIGER

Black stripes camouflage it in the bushes
Bone white teeth shining in the dark
Eyes sparkling at prey
Pouncing ferociously at dinner
Bellies rumbling throughout the day
Purring silently as it stalks animals
Claws digging in the ground
Getting ready to pounce.

Kevin Gater (10)
Brookwood Primary School

WITCHES' SPELLS

Eye of a frog
Tongue of a dog
Spirits cry, ''Tis time, 'tis time.'
Round and round the cauldron goes
Double bubble, toil and trouble.

Sweated venom, sleeping goat
Cry of baby from the cot
Leaf of blood although the flood
Double bubble, toil and trouble.

Tail of a rat, wool of a bat
Tooth of a cat
Prick of a cactus
Double bubble, toil and trouble.

Ha, ha, ha, ha, ha.

Natalie Luke (11)
Brookwood Primary School

INSIDE MY HEAD

Inside my head is a matrix of rocky caves,
Carpeted with diamonds and lined with fire,
And deep, deep down at the bottom of my head lies a lake,
A deep, dark lake of acid and evil,
Only three things live in my head;
Evil, a fiery monster roaming freely,
A genie, trapped in a lamp,
And angels getting nowhere on their sparkling wings.

John Lugton (11)
Brookwood Primary School

WATER, WATER EVERYWHERE

Uh-oh, here comes the rain,
Splashing on my windowpane,
Splish-splosh on the ground,
Making such a funny sound.

More and more from the sky,
Up, up so very high,
Will it ever stop,
We ask with every drop.

The ground is wet,
The weather has set,
The rivers are high,
I give another enormous sigh.

At last the clouds part,
At least that's a start!
A ray of sun appears,
The whole school lets out *three big cheers*.

Amy Lorman-Parker (10)
Brookwood Primary School

MY HEAD

Inside my head are secret thoughts never to be told,
Are messages which tell me what to do,
Inside my head I am seeing things which only I know are there,
I am far away, in a different world than you.

Outside my head are people who love to chat and play,
Are things I want to see and know or talk to everyday,
Are things which I love to see and do and people that I can trust.

Fiona Thornton (10)
Brookwood Primary School

MATILDA

Matilda had such a super brain,
And oh how her brother was such a big pain
Who thought that Matilda knew nothing at all,
Until she had started Miss Trunchbull's old school.
Matilda's first teacher was young, nice Miss Honey,
And Matilda agreed that this was worth the money.
Matilda's first friend was called Lavender Brown,
Who lived quite far away down in the town.
Matilda and Lavender had so much fun,
They spent hours and hours playing in the sun.

Then one dull day they went out to play,
And they found a small newt on their way.
Then the next day they went to their school,
And that's where they found out the new rule
About not bringing pets into their class,
So Matilda emptied the newt out into a glass.
Then in through the door Miss Trunchbull came,
Looking like usual (just the same).
Miss Trunchbull sat down and picked up the glass,
Staring out of her cold dark eyes at the class.
Then when she picked up the glass of icy water,
She came eye to eye with the newt,
And screamed without falter!

Louisa Mousley (10)
Brookwood Primary School

THE OCTOBER STORM

I wake up
Listen to the noises of the night.
The wind is howling
The thunder is growling.
I gasp,
The window is creaking.
The trees are cracking.
Bang
Goes the apple tree!
I hear the gutter squeaking
And the rain beating on the roof.
I go back to sleep.

I wake up again.
Hear a crashing sound.
I run to my mum and dad's room
Just in time,
For a tree fell in my room.
I wake them.
And then,
Bang!
A tree fell,
Blocking the doorway.
I look out the window
And see
The leaves swirling,
And hear
Next door's baby crying.
I grab the phone,
Dial 999.
They come
To take us to safety.

Sophie Hobbs (10)
Brookwood Primary School

A Dark Stormy Night

Gates were squeaking
Doors were creaking
Cars in crashes
Making bashes
The rain was pouring
I was yawning
It would flood me out
Without a doubt
My mum was asleep
My dad was in a heap
When I was thinking what to do
The wind was howling, 'Boo hoo hoo'
What I don't understand
Is why it felt so grand
On this dark and stormy night?

Sophie Gilby (9)
Brookwood Primary School

The October Storm

One stormy night
All I heard
Was windows smashing
Falling branches
Trees creaking
Rain bashing
Dogs howling
Cats meowing
Babies crying
Boats rowing
Cars crashing
How I wish the night would end.

Robert Devine (9)
Brookwood Primary School

WITCHES' SPELL

Two slimy rats' guts
with some little mutts.
One tiger's heart
and that's just the start.
Four stinky pigs' brains
make sure they're tame.
Twelve eyes from men
make that ten.
Throw in some blood
and the mud of a flood.
A pair of woman's eyes
and two custard pies.
A dung beetle with a handful of dung,
throw in a German shepherd's tongue.
A daddy-long-legs that has died.
Throw in a tarantula that is alive.
Two goldfish fins.
Four old litter bins.
Throw in some mice,
won't that be nice?
One giraffe's neck.
A piece of deck.
An elephant's tooth
with a ticket booth.
One bleeding leg
make sure they didn't beg.
One small dog's tail
which had failed.

Bethany Goodway (10)
Brookwood Primary School

HURRICANE

Hurricane, hurricane
Such a big pain
Hurricane, hurricane
It came from the west
Hurricane, hurricane
It was a very big pest
It came to my town
It scared me a lot
Lots fell down
Hurricane, hurricane
It came with a force
For all to see
It stayed on course
And blew down the trees
Hurricane, hurricane.

Hurricane, hurricane
Tossing the big ships out on the sea,
Like Frisbees in the sky
You great big bully
Making us cry
Nothing and no one is safe from a hurricane
Expect the moles in their holes
Or the stars in the sky
Hurricane, hurricane
Go away
Your work is done
This time of day
Hurricane, hurricane.

Adam Stovold (8)
Goldsworth Primary School

Sssssssnake!

He is the master of disguise,
He can blend in perfectly with his surroundings
Like a chameleon . . .
Snake!

He moves like a ghost,
Hovering smoothly
Through long grass,
Like death,
Following his prey . . .
Stealthy, sly, slithering snake!

He slips and slides through the long grass,
He is the jungle's spy,
An all-seeing eye . . .
Stealthy snake!

He seems to know everything,
All the jungle's secrets,
Where the rats hide,
Where he can breakfast,
But he never shares his knowledge . . .
Stealthy, sly, slithering, snake.

He knows that he is flight delimited, but
Sometimes he wishes to be a hawk!
He would grow wings, flap them,
Fly up into the air; soar high in the sky,
And silently plummet down,
Crushing his prey -
That stealthy, sly, slithering, shifty . . .
Snake!

Henry Stanley (11)
Goldsworth Primary School

The Owl

Its eyes like scorches
Its pupils bigger than its claws
Its beak like stone
At night he's gone
Defying gravity at best
His feathered vest
His ears on end
On the lookout for prey
He sees his prey
He hears his prey
He swoops down,
Down, down and down again
And finally
With half a tail in its mouth
It sits on a branch
Thinking with glee
How wonderful it would be
To be a bee
Not being seen
Not being heard
Going in stealth
And rolling in wealth.

Gareth Musgrove (11)
Goldsworth Primary School

Dolphins

Dolphins swimming, splish, splash
Dolphins swerving, splash, splish
Dolphins jumping, splash, splosh
Swimming with dolphins, splish, splash.

Rosie Kingston (8)
Goldsworth Primary School

SNAKE

Coiled up like a spring
Ready to strike!

Twisting and turning like liquorice lace
Writhing, wriggling prey tries to escape.

Twisting, turning, struggling.
But the mouse surrenders.
The venomous fangs get the better of it
And the hunter swallows it whole.

But what's this?

Slithering its forked tongue in and out.
Hungry for more.

It coils up like a spring
Ready to strike!

Tanya Lattul (11)
Goldsworth Primary School

DOLPHINS ARE MY ONLY FRIENDS

Dolphins are my only friends,
And they will be right to the end!

Gliding through the sea,
As happy as could be,
Why don't you glide with me?

Dolphins are my only friends,
And they will be right to the end!

Stephanie Evans (9)
Goldsworth Primary School

WHISPER
(For Whisper the horse)

Swish swish like the sea rocking is Whisper's tail.
Her body like a shadow, slender and sleek - Whisper.

Her movement flows, like the rushing wind - Whisper.
Her muzzle like velvet - smooth and soft.

Her mane flies freely like a bird.
Gracefully she prances in the sunlight.

She soars through the air like a golden eagle - Whisper.
Racing the wind and then gone.

Sophie Etter (11)
Goldsworth Primary School

THUNDER!

Clip-clopping along,
The horse is singing a song,
Smooth, soft, sleek coat,
There with him was a goat.

His twinkling eyes are brown,
There he was wearing a crown.
He glitters in the light of the sun,
There he gallops to his mum.

His foam-white mane
And tail shines in the light of the moon.
He gallops to the water,
His reflection is still and calm.

Nashmia Zubair (10)
Goldsworth Primary School

DOLPHIN

Swimming in the sea
Playing games happily - the dolphin
Bobbing in and out the air
Looking around he likes to stare - the dolphin

Shining like a star in the sky
Splashing around people getting wet - the dolphin
Swimming so fast like a jet
Catching fish, getting happy - the dolphin

The day is over, all had fun
Resting calm and still - the dolphin
The water, quiet and peaceful
Night comes at least to the dolphin.

Beth McCready (11)
Goldsworth Primary School

MY CAT

Miaow, miaow goes my cat,
Waiting for her food.
Miaow, miaow goes my cat,
I can't find my shoes.
Miaow, miaow goes my cat,
I need to buy some more cat food.
Miaow, miaow goes my cat,
I just found my shoes.
Miaow, miaow goes my cat,
I went to the supermarket.
When I got home, surprise, surprise
My cat didn't want her food!

Aleesha Sharma (8)
Goldsworth Primary School

GREGORY

A moving tree
The king of the world - Gregory

The one with the neck
Soaring up to the sky - Gregory

Pulling down trees
One at a time - Gregory

With its smooth tongue
Sucks out the moisture
Of the branches up high

Gregory survives without water
Does not need a drink
One after the other he pulls down and eats leaves
He has no voice but you can still hear him.

Because of this reason, he really wants to be;
A laughing monkey swinging in a tree . . .
Or maybe an ant
Still sucking the moisture out of the leaves.

William Phelan (11)
Goldsworth Primary School

CATS

The tamed animal
So tamed as a mammal
So very, very fierce
As fierce as a fire
He swallowed his prey
His prey gurgled as he lay
His coat as orange as the sun.

Rebecca Carter (11)
Goldsworth Primary School

INSECTS

Ants in the bathroom
Spiders in the lounge
Worms in the basement
And this is what I found.

Slugs in the hallway
Flies on the floor
Snails in my bedroom
And this is what I saw.

Maggots on the window ledge
Glow-worms in the porch
Ladybirds in the dining room
I can't take it anymore!

Woodlouse on the driveway
Cockroach in the study
Moths in the playroom
Eating Chinese curry!

Amy Kingston (11)
Goldsworth Primary School

LIFE OF AN ANT

I'm in the grass all day,
During the day I scramble for safety.
There's a big foot coming, boom, boom, boom!
Coming through the grass village.
Help, help, we shout!
In the night we snuggle up to the lovely warm grass.

Stewart Lifton (8)
Goldsworth Primary School

THE EARTHQUAKE

The earth beneath my feet
Began to shake
Trembling with anger
The earth was starting to eat
Devouring everything in sight
The houses crumpled
Before my very eyes
As if they were made out of paper
In the distance
I could hear wails and cries
Of people in desperate need
People were trapped under the rubble
Screeching out for help
Oh God, what have we done
To deserve so much trouble
Please God, save us
As the tremors subside
A ravaged landscape is left behind
Which was once so full of pride
Their lives would never be the same again.

Komil Sarwar (10)
Goldsworth Primary School

SWIMMING IN THE SEA

Splash! Splash goes a dolphin.
A dolphin swimming round and around me.
Wave your tail at me and sing to me.
Splash! Splash! Splosh goes a dolphin!
Dolphins are great and fun to play with.

I love dolphins!

Luke Butcher (9)
Goldsworth Primary School

PEOPLE WHO HELP US

When there's a robbery,
A car accident or something like that,
Who comes to help us?
The police.

When there's a fire,
An overflow of water or something like that,
Who comes to help us?
The fire brigade.

When someone's ill,
Or badly injured or something like that,
Who comes to help us?
The ambulance crew.

When someone wants to cross the road,
Stop the traffic or something like that,
Who comes to help us?
The lollipop lady.

Richard Tervet (8)
Goldsworth Primary School

ALIEN POWER

Some aliens landed on Earth - hissssssss!
They launched two rockets- Boom! Boom!
They fired their lazer guns - Zap! Zap!
They threw smoke bombs - ssssssss.
They threw gas bombs - Cough! Cough!
They hit people on the head with clubs and books.
'What a life,' a man said, 'what a life!'

Hector Stanley (8)
Goldsworth Primary School

WOULDN'T IT BE FUNNY?

Wouldn't it be funny if a cow went woof,
And a dog went moo?
Wouldn't it be funny if a clock went neigh,
And a horse went tick?
Wouldn't it be funny if a bomb went wobble,
And jelly went bang?
Wouldn't it be funny if a grown-up went goo-gaga,
And a baby went, you naughty boy?
Wouldn't it be funny if crisps went fizz,
And cola went crunch?
Wouldn't it be funny?
Well, wouldn't it be funny?
Well, wouldn't it be funny like that?

Simon Brown (9)
Goldsworth Primary School

DOLPHINS

Click, click,
Is that a dolphin?
Ee, eee,
Of course it is!
Click, click,
Watch them swish their tails!
Ee, eee,
Let's swim with them
Click, click,
They're beautiful
Ee, eee.

Kirstin Hay (9)
Goldsworth Primary School

My Amazing Pet Tiger

My amazing pet tiger roars,
roar, roar.
You hear his roaring all around the jungle,
roar, roar.

My amazing pet tiger eats meat,
crunch, crunch.
He eats tons of it each day,
crunch, crunch.

My amazing pet tiger is heavy,
weight lifter, weight lifter.
He needs lots of people to lift him,
weight lifter, weight lifter.

Hannah Davidson (9)
Goldsworth Primary School

A Rainy Day

The rain falls, down on walls,

drip, drop,
drip, drop.

The rain dives into beehives,

drip, drop,
drip, drop.

When it stops, I can play outside,

sunshine,
sunshine.

Leah Bray
Goldsworth Primary School

WHAT A NOISE!

Roar, roar,
Roaring tigers.

Hiss, hiss,
Hissing snakes.

Snap, snap,
Snapping crocodiles.

Stomp, stomp,
Stomping elephants.

Quack, quack,
Quacking ducks.

Bark, bark,
Barking dogs.

Roar, roar, hiss, hiss, snap, snap,
Stomp, stomp, quack, quack, bark, bark.

What a noise!

Amelia Skerritt (9)
Goldsworth Primary School

TRAMPOLINING

Bouncing on a trampoline
High and low
Reach for the sky
So go, go, go
Doing a star jump
Stretch your legs
Point your fingers
Like little pegs.

Alex Follett (9)
Goldsworth Primary School

MAGICAL MOONLIGHT

I was up in the sky as high as the moon
The stars were sparkling above the houses
People in their homes fast asleep
The streets quiet as a mouse

No sound, no whisper or no cry
Just the moon shining across the sky
The silvery, bright and magical stars
Lighting up the darkness around

I am moving like a ghost in the sleepy shadows
No one can see me in this dreamy world
No one can hear my heart beating like a drum
This is a place I can call my home.

I am swirling around the glittery sky
I feel like an angel flying so high
I wish everyone could see this fabulous place
This is what I call a magical moonlight.

Henna Irshad (9)
Goldsworth Primary School

MY DOLPHIN SPLASHES

My dolphin splashes in the sea like this - splish-splash.
I go to the sea and I swim like a shark.
I wonder what I would do without the dolphins.
My dolphin goes splishety-splash, splish-splash.
My dolphin makes a noise like this - eeeh!
My dolphin sounds like a little mouse.

Samman Nawaz (8)
Goldsworth Primary School

My Dolphin

I have a friend named Chloe,
She's my best mate,
We always hang out together whether it's early or late,
She's the one I go to whether I'm happy or sad,
Or when I've been good or bad.
I think she's really cool
And there's one place that I wish I could take her and that is *school*!
I always tell people at school about Chloe, they never believe me,
Just wait, they'll see.
I can rely on my pet,
She knows that I'll never try and catch her or put her in a net.

Emma Rashbrook (9)
Goldsworth Primary School

The Bell Goes Wrong

Bing bong
It's eleven o'clock and the bell goes wrong
They thought it would be very strong.

The bell goes bing and bell goes bong.

The bell goes tick
The bell goes tock.
That's not right
That is the clock's tock

Bing bong, the bell goes wrong
It's five o'clock, not midnight.

Marco Cala (9)
Goldsworth Primary School

23

THE TORTOISE

His body protected by a shield
straining to see.

Small and studious
carrying his home on his back.

Softly and slowly galumping along
thinking to himself if he were a monkey . . .

He could run, win races, beat all sorts of paces.
leap from tree to tree and eat bananas,
as much as he please,
it would be a change from eating nuts and grains.

Monkeys can scavenge far and wide,
seeking food for their hungry insides.
Try to compare . . .
You cannot.

Madeleine King (10)
Goldsworth Primary School

WIND

You are so swift,
You are so cool,
You are so gentle,
You are so calm,
You are so kind,
You are so rarely rough,
You are so soft,
You are wind!

Mark Flewitt (8)
Goldsworth Primary School

ORANG-UTAN

Old man of the forest,
New man of the zoo.
He does not quite fit in
As does the lion or the elephant.
He longs for freedom and his family
And to get rid of the horrid bars
He curses them and bites them
As they block his path.

His shaggy orange coat
No longer gleams and shines
But is greyish and dull.

His voice no longer bellows and bawls
But is as silent as a mouse
He hides away in the straw
Away from the glare of the sun
And flashing cameras.

The orang-utan, once old man of the forest,
Now new man of the zoo.

Ben Matthews (10)
Goldsworth Primary School

DOLPHINS

Dolphins jumping, splish, splash
Dolphins swimming, splish, splash
Dolphins playing, splish, splash
Dolphins chasing, splish, splash
Dolphins jerking, splish, splash
Dolphins splashing, splish, splash
Dolphins leaping, splish, splash.

Joe Ensoll (9)
Goldsworth Primary School

RAIN

I am locked inside
Pitter-patter
Pitter-patter
I don't know what to do
Pitter-patter
Pitter-patter
I am going to do a puzzle
Pitter-patter
Pitter-patter
I am going to read a book
Pitter-patter
Pitter-patter
I am going to do my homework
Pitter-patter
Pitter-patter
It is time for bed!
Pitter-patter
Pitter-patter.

Ellie Davey (8)
Goldsworth Primary School

MY HORSE

Galloping round the yard,
clip-clop.
Blowing a whistle
so you come towards me
clip-clop.
Gleaming chestnut coat
clip-clop.
Let's go out for a ride
clip-clop.

Stephanie Holden (8)
Goldsworth Primary School

Lucy's Explosive Bomb

There once was a girl called Lucy
Who decided to build an explosive bomb, code named 'Juicy',
But then her friend decided to help,
Who had a hideous pink belt,
They both decided to add some milk,
But the strange thing was, they added some silk.
To make it worse they added some glue.
First they tried some water,
They even thought of flying to mortar,
(But of course they weren't allowed)
Then they tried some butter,
But all the flies went flutter,
The only thing was, when the bomb went bang
And the metal went clang
That was the end of that.

Holly Taylor (10)
Goldsworth Primary School

My Hamster

My hamster was the best pet I ever had.
And when he died one morning I was so sad.
My world was turned upside down.
I'll always remember his coat so brown
And how he so enjoyed his special pen.
How he curled up in his den.
One morning we came down to breakfast
And he was in his tank.
He died in my hand,
And nothing will replace him,
Not all the gold in the land.

Christopher Lodge (10)
Goldsworth Primary School

IF I WERE BIG

Verse 1
   If I were big, I would not be
   A diplomat like my daddy,
   I wouldn't be a plumber,
   I wouldn't mend the pipes,
   I wouldn't be an electrician,
   I wouldn't mend the lights,
   No, they're not jobs for me.

Chorus
   Cos if I were big,
   I'd rather be a big policeman
   That's what I'd be,
   That's the job for me,
   But only when I'm big!

Verse 2
   If I were big I wouldn't be
   A London worker, in the big city,
   I wouldn't be a pilot,
   I would not fly a lot,
   No, they're not jobs for me!

Chorus

Verse 3
   If I were big, I wouldn't take
   A job in a garden,
   Or a job by a lake,
   Not a doctor, not a nurse,
   I can think of nothing worse,
   All that gore, all that blood
   I would rather work in mud.

Chorus

    I'll just be a policeman
    Yep, that's me!

Craig Ellis (9)
Goldsworth Primary School

WHAT LOVELY ANIMALS!

Dogs are so lovely,
Their fur is so tickly,
They're so soft and sweet,
What lovely animals!
Dolphins are so lovely,
They splash around all day,
Everyone will say for sure
What lovely animals!
Cats are so lovely,
Their purring is like magic,
If only they could speak to me,
What lovely animals!
Horses are so lovely,
Their tails are like silky hair,
Their hooves beat down
On the ground,
What lovely animals!

I love all animals,
They're all so sweet,
I love them so much,
What lovely animals!

Meriam Ahmed (9)
Goldsworth Primary School

LILY PAD

Silky black and snowy white is Lily Pad.

Sitting still, she nibbles at her favourite food -
Bamboo.

As shy as a mouse, she moves slowly
To her home in the tree trunk.

Her fur feels like velvet and her eyes
Are like a puppy wanting food.

So sweet is Lily Pad
As she is a very rare baby.

The shade of the trees cool Lily Pad
And her mother from the warm Asian sun.

Eleanor Wilmott (11)
Goldsworth Primary School

DRUM

Cymbals clash,
And the drum will crash.
Rat-a-tat-tat,
Bash, crash, smash.
Music all night long.
Pat, pat goes the beat,
Pat-a-pat-pat.
Now the drums go back
Under cloth till tomorrow evening.

Joseph Grilli (8)
Goldsworth Primary School

UNDER THE SEA

I was under the deep turquoise sea,
Beautiful starfish and coral reef
All different colours; blues, greens and golds,
The thing that caught my eye
Was a beautiful, sleek dolphin
Swimming gracefully through the coral,
Flipping up and down.
She swam up to the surface,
I followed her and came to the surface,
I saw her jump up and down.
She waved goodbye with her tail,
A splash of water fell on my face,
As she somersaulted away into the distance.

Emma Riddell (10)
Goldsworth Primary School

MY BOOTS

My boots go tap, tap
In the daytime,
Tap, tap at night-time,
Tap, tap at handwriting,
Tap, tap at dance class,
Tap, tap at piano practice,
Tap, tap at play time.
All that my boots do
Is go tap, tap, tap,
All year round.

Charlotte Oswick (8)
Goldsworth Primary School

THE FOUR SEASONS

Spring
The spring bulbs are budding
The colours are bright
The days are much longer
And shorter the night.

Summer
Picnics and barbies
Days come alive
The birds sing happily
Bees buzz round the hive.

Autumn
The trees in the autumn
Are so bare
The leaves have all fallen
And are scattered everywhere.

Winter
The north wind is blowing
The year has nearly gone
But the bright lights of Christmas
Brings joy to everyone.

Annabel McKnespiey (8)
Goldsworth Primary School

POLAR BEAR

Arctic animal
Wild and free,
Doesn't know that he would be
Locked up in a cage.
Endangered beauty,
What a shame,
No more snow for him to see.

Cute and cuddly,
No more ice,
Slow and steady, like a snail.
Arctic animal,
Free again,
Sleeps on ice,
Finally away.

Amber Lay (10)
Goldsworth Primary School

MIDNIGHT

My feet were cold as I lay in bed
and scary thoughts ran through my head.
My body froze, my lips were dry,
the house was quiet and I wondered why?
The moving shadows gave me a fright.
Petrified, I closed my eyes tight.
But that didn't help because I saw
a creepy burglar at the door.
I opened my eyes and looked at the blind,
was the light playing tricks on my mind?
My heart stopped, my body froze,
when I saw a great big nose
pressed up against the windowpane,
that burglar was back again.
I jumped out of my bed and ran to my mum,
I pleaded but she wouldn't come.
She pulled back the duvet and in I crept,
and next to my mum I safely slept.
In the morning my courage was back,
my fear was gone from the midnight attack.
But at bedtime once again
would that nose be at the windowpane?

Jennifer Clarke (9)
Goldsworth Primary School

THE DAY I SLID DOWN THE DRAIN

The day I slid down the drain
Was a very big pain,
I will always remember that day,
I hope I didn't clog up the pipes or else I'd have to pay,

Then suddenly a spout of dirt came down,
So I ran as fast as wind with a frown,
Soon after, a swarm of stinky rubbish came down the drain
Which was the same, as the horrible thing that tasted like mud,
I had for dinner last week,
Then I screamed that sounded like a big mouse's squeak,

But that surprised me, because it made me go faster
And faster down the very stinky drain,
Then I saw my very old and dusty teddy bear called Fame,
So I cried and cried because his head came off,
That made me go even faster down the pipe,
With stripes,

But it stank bad to worse, in the pipe more than six skunks,
Then I reached the sea that was full of drunk punks,
Drinking beer, they will probably get diarrhoea,
But how will I ever get home I thought!
Suddenly I saw a bit of a fort,

But the rest had sank,
And I still stank,
Still I climbed up the drain,
Then I came,

Home sweet home!

Tanya Advani (9)
Goldsworth Primary School

MATHS LESSON

1, 2, 3, 4, I got bored in my maths lesson, while
James recited his 13 times table
and Vanessa wrote 88 sums
when we found out Jonathan cheated in maths.

Chorus
Maths, maths, what will I do,
I don't learn a thing and neither will you.

5, 6, 7, 8, I was really getting bored by this time, while
Zac, Adam and Fraser got started reading mathematical jokes,
while Craig listened to what Jenny had to say,
and Emma told all the answers to Gemma.

Chorus

9, 10, 11, 12, by this time I was bored to death, while
Ammy taught Chloe aand Alex to count to 100,000,000
Abby and Charlotte figured out the 17 times table,
and Jared became the man with the plan.

Chorus

13, 14, 15, 16, in fact I was dead with boredom, while,
Georgina told Najma the 18 times table,
and Rebecca helped Rebecca,
while Sherry, Henna, Rubia and Sanya
answered the question for Daniel.

Chorus

17, 18, 19, 20, by now I was the haunted ghost of boredom,
While Miles chattered to Brendon,
and Kevin wrote numbers on his BB gun.

Claire Bowerman (8)
Goldsworth Primary School

DELIGHTFUL DECEMBER

December wakes up to look out the window and
Finds frosty jewel-like dew covering the grass
Then goes downstairs as bold as brass.
The snow falls down upon the ground,
Like a blizzard of flour spinning around.
The trees are bare, the grass is white.
December is full of joyful delight.
When he enters his warm, cosy home,
He doesn't feel too alone.
He warms his feet and frozen hands,
Unlike many people from warmer lands.
So when the summer has finally come
He warms himself out in the sun.

Lianne Saunders (10)
Goldsworth Primary School

IF I WERE

If I were small
I would go to Play School
Without a pool
I would sit in the high chair
Without much hair
I would play with toys
And make a lot of noise.

If I were big
I wouldn't be a pilot
And cause a riot
I wouldn't be a taxi driver
And get paid a fiver
I wouldn't be a vet
And cure lots of pets.

Jonathan Boxall (9)
Goldsworth Primary School

MY DOG

My dog is sandy brown
With long, floppy ears that dangle down
He's got sweet dark brown eyes
That have never told lies

My dog loves to have fun
And never lets me get anything done
He's got a long, wiggly tail
Which blows about like a sail

My dog is very fat
Because he always sits on the door mat
He's got great big paws
That leave marks on doors

But he is still the best dog in the world!

Shehryar Sarwar (8)
Goldsworth Primary School

FLANNAN ISLE

We stared and we stared at the food left there
And at the ghostly, upturned ivory chair,
While outside the strange birds hovered there.
We heard a ghostly, whispering voice which
Seemed to whisper ever more.
We looked around at the walls, blood-red
And at the blood-stained oak wood bed
For in it there was a green-eyed head,
Eyes that looked out of the window
At the labyrinth of the cloudy skies,
With its body by its side.
And still outside the strange birds hovered
Like gods of the underworld.
Then with wings of golden light
They opened their rake-like talons
And landed on the broken roof.
Like gargoyles they sat,
Leering at us with evil eyes
As we stared and stared with fright.
We stared and stared until time seemed to halt
And the clocks stood still
And the light in our lives seemed to fade.
We all felt like running but were rooted with fear.
Behind us the doors closed as day became night
And the grandfather clock read midnight.
We opened the doors and ran with great haste
To our boat 'Grace'.
Then we sailed away for a year and a day
To our homes in the Great South Bay
Never to return to the evil place again.

Alex Paterson (10)
Goldsworth Primary School

SNAKES

Slimy snakes, slimy snakes slither around in the dirty lakes.
They're over here and they're over there,
You'd better run or they will give you a scare,
They eat rats and they're scared of bats,
And of course their worst enemies are . . .
Cats!

Daniel Barbato (8)
Goldsworth Primary School

STARS

Stars come out
when you're asleep
or counting sheep

Stars come out
when you're in bed
snug with ted.

Stars go down
when the sun
comes up and
you get up

Yes you
get up!

Rebecca Evans (9)
Goldsworth Primary School

THE LION

The lion full of pride with his huge giant head
Surrounded by his bright yellow, shaggy mane,
Tearing around the long, green and grassy plains,
Suddenly pouncing on his prey, the zebra,
He roars with so much pride and honour
As he invites the rest of his pride to dinner.
Pounding for another one or maybe not the same
She walks round and round ready for her prey,
Quietly, she waits patiently for a small young gazelle,
Suddenly she charges in a quick and fast dazzle,
But this quickly escapes
And she, the female lion walks away in shame.

Louise Cook (11)
Goldsworth Primary School

RIVER BANK

Beside the river bank
I like to sit and talk,
Inside the armoured tank
My friends like to come.
We hang around and listen,
We think it makes us calm,
Then we watch the water glisten.
As we were listening
The wind was whistling
Through the trees and leaves.

Rebecca Sullivan (10)
Goldsworth Primary School

PANDA

The bamboo-eater,
Plump, black and white panda.
Her human-like hands eat ravenously,
She's an endangered animal,
Her life is forever at risk.
Her tired looking eyes are dark,
Almost black with panic,
Her body is as cuddly as a teddy bear,
She would beautifully match a zebra crossing,
With her gorgeous black and white coat,
Her coat feels smooth like newly varnished wood.
One day she wishes to be a butterfly,
And fly away to safety.

Elizabeth Turnbull (10)
Goldsworth Primary School

AN ELEGY OF MY GRANDAD

Whenever I remember
When my grandad died in December
I felt my world had ended.
My mum was crying,
When my grandad was dying,
I was only a child.
As my mum was going wild
My dad was so sad,
He felt very bad,
When my grandad died in December.

Lucy Lord (10)
Goldsworth Primary School

SUMMER

Summer is great you should like it more than anything.
You can play ball and do it with a ping.
In the sun it's as bright as a tight.
But when it rains it becomes very light.
Summer is great, the days are long.
Playing outside is great fun. *Pong*!
Play in the park, on the swing can be great fun.
Especially with a great big currant bun.
'Come on in' calls Mother 'have your tea and then baths.'
After the sun goes down the children go to bed
Goodnight, sleep tight.

Sahnya Razaq (8)
Goldsworth Primary School

WHALES

Large, magnificent, intelligent animals are whales
Whales are mammals not fish
Spend all their time in the water
Largest and loudest animals on the Earth
The height of a nine storey building is a whale
Many whales are acrobats
Whale songs can be heard miles under the water
Smallest whale is the dwarf whale
Biggest whale is the blue whale.

Laura Holdaway (10)
Goldsworth Primary School

PLEASE MR POLICEMAN

Please Mr Policeman,
arrest that girl,
she stole my house,
and that was over £100,000.

Please Mr Policeman,
arrest that boy,
he stole my laptop and 24
of my favourite tapes.

Please Mr Policeman
arrest that man,
he stole my cheque.
£200 on that cheque.
I say, so be a good lad
and arrest that man
that was standing there a minute ago.

Gemma Tong (8)
Goldsworth Primary School

LIONS

A lion is a sandy yellow
Which seems to beam with the sun.
He runs with great importance.
They watch cautiously to find their prey.
They kill and eat zebras and giraffes.
Baby lions have dark spots on their sides.

Rebecca Pateman (11)
Goldsworth Primary School

SCHOOL

Goldsworth School is the best
Better than all the best of the rest
All the teachers are so cool
At fantastic Goldsworth school
Mrs Smith is so kind
Leaving Mum we don't mind
Miss O'Brien is full of fun
Especially for year one
Mrs Webber takes the other class
I hear her as I pass
Mrs Brewer you will like
Give her a wave when she's on her bike
Behave yourself for Miss Browning
Or else she will end up frowning
Mrs Jones takes year three
A very good teacher don't you agree?
When you're in year three and it's time for P.E.
It's off to the big hall with Miss Lacey
When listening to Miss Till
Make sure you sit very still
Mrs Lloyd-Hitt takes year four
Her name is on the classroom door
Mrs Broadly takes year five
To teach you French she must strive
Miss Hopkins teaches us netball
Perhaps it's because she's so tall
Mrs Bamford teaches year six classes
In her test she likes good passes
Mrs Thomas is new to this school
She was amazed at the swimming pool

Mrs Alexander is our Head
Her stories are well read
That's the staff of Goldsworth school
Now you have met them all.

Rebecca Piggott (8)
Goldsworth Primary School

GIRAFFE

The supply, lofty
leaf killer awaits.
Her body's as thin
as a pin and you
would think she
was 2D.
Her long, towering
neck extends to
peek over the highest
treetops.
Her eyes elegantly
watch over everything.
Her feet prolonged all
the way up to her hips.
Her hips stick out like
a gutter on a house.
Her skin, patches of
brown against yellow.
The feeling's smooth.
She slowly moves but
gracefully, she ponders
about sprinting to search
for her family.
Oh, she wishes that day would come.

Alison Sayers (10)
Goldsworth Primary School

TIGER

His gentle eyes and soft fur,
He protects his territory,
Big and cuddly, but don't get too close,
One . . . two . . . three . . . pounce!
When he pounces his prey are in defeat,
King of attacks,
Graceful hunter,
Silent mover,
Careful paws, not a sound,
Big kitten, lying on the ground,
The sun glaring down on him,
Until he's hungry once more,
His roar, like a siren warning others away!

Emma Whitehead (10)
Goldsworth Primary School

BAT

Darkness . . . silence . . .
Quick, small watcher . . .
Waiter . . .
Night hunter, like an arrow in the dark . . .
Agile as the wind . . .
King of the nightmare hour . . .
Ruler of the shadows . . .
He is . . . *the bat*!

Gabriel McLoughlin (10)
Goldsworth Primary School

TREE FROG

His skin makes him a frog not to miss,
He is very bright to look at,
His eyes are big like beady marbles,
His feet are different colours!
He sits waiting to catch his prey,
Crunch!
He caught a fly,
A tree frog could kill a monkey,
When he is still he's like plastic,
Still catching his prey or not
He will sit watching on the same old rock.

Emma Denty (10)
Goldsworth Primary School

DOG

Arm-licker . . . hand tiring . . .
Burglar-cruncher . . . shoe wetter . . .
His name is Thomas.
He'll sit calmly by the sitting room chair
Letting your hand go back and forth
Over his rough gold fur . . .
But take him outside and he will run around
Chasing tennis balls and sticks.
He is as quick as a jaguar when he's outside.
He's as clever as a young human . . .
He is the best,
His name is Thomas and he's a dog.

Ben Grilli (10)
Goldsworth Primary School

THE GREAT WHITE SHARK

Fierce, fast, deadly, cruel, vicious,
Mean, sneaky, giant, clever and strong.
The great white shark moves as fast as a rocket
On full blast to catch its prey.
Teeth as sharp as knives and white as snow.
His nickname is the man-eater.
His name is Jaws.
Destroys everything in sight.
As strong as a hundred pound stone.
His colour is as grey as smoke.
When he sees you he chases and chases you
Until he gets you, then *chomp* goes his mouth,
And you are left in his belly.

Daniel Addison (10)
Goldsworth Primary School

JAGUAR

Jaguar - the spotted king of South America.
Jaguar - with eyes like marbles,
It shoots like a bullet after its victim
And makes its graceful impression
With its cheerless gloomy coat.
If you ever approach this beast,
You will wish you never had.
Then he had an idea -
He could become a butterfly and fly far away,
He could be free.

Ben Moss (11)
Goldsworth Primary School

THE CHEETAH

With his grace and gifted speed
He has no worries and no morals
His evil glare will cut straight through you
He is proud with no interest for anyone else

On the prowl he will always be watching . . .
Waiting . . . to pounce
You will not see him, you will not hear him
Each claw is like a tiny scythe,
Sharp enough to rip a carcass apart.
He looks down on all other animals
For he is truly the king of the jungle.

Ben Peppitt (10)
Goldsworth Primary School

PANTHER

He spots his prey,
He leaps, gliding gracefully through the air,
Like an arrow,
The night shadow leaps to the ground,
His prey is gone,
Nowhere to be found,
So once more he returns to his tree,
His velvety fur glimmers in the sun,
He bares his teeth ready to pounce.

Sarah Piggott (10)
Goldsworth Primary School

Foxy The Fox

The night animal,
The speeding, fluffy night animal . . . the fox.
His name is Foxy, the dangerous, sly, sneaky animal.
He has long endless whiskers like the endless sky.
His gazing eyes watching his prey.
He can hear almost anything with his long pointy ears.
His paws as round and as small as bouncy balls.
Suddenly, he moves slowly, watching his prey.
He pounces and has caught his dinner.

Emma Colbourn (10)
Goldsworth Primary School

Black King Cobra

Black king cobra - stranger than any human,
dextrous and fearless.
Black king cobra - eyes like shining black diamonds,
its hood opens when in terror only.
As long as a steam train at full speed.
The poison in his fangs gives a vital advantage
over his victim.
Cold-blooded black king cobra,
he waits till this very day.

Ashwin Sharma (11)
Goldsworth Primary School

POP STARS

All those pop stars on TV
When I grow up that's what I want to be
Singing on their glittering stages
Plus they get excellent wages
But when they sing an awful tune
I change the channel and watch a cartoon
I like Britney and Billie
Eminem as well? Don't be silly!
Listening to music is my hobby
But not that awful builder Bobby
Pop stars are cool, pop stars are great
I wish Britney Spears was my best mate!

Vanessa Baquer (9)
Goldsworth Primary School

SCHOOL

It's cool to be at school!
Art is the best
I'm not sure about the rest,
History's OK
It leads the way,
Maths is the worst
I'm sure it's cursed!
Connectives and similes . . .
English is so great
It makes me think straight!
In PE I have fun
I run and run,
Yes, it's cool to be at school.

Georgina Melville (9)
Goldsworth Primary School

DINOSAURS COMING

Dinosaurs coming
Watch and beware.
Dinosaurs coming
You're in for a scare.
Dinosaurs coming
You're in for a fright.
Dinosaurs coming
He wants a bite.
Dinosaurs coming
He is after you.
Dinosaurs coming
What will you do?
Dinosaurs coming
He is roaring at you.
Dinosaurs coming
Your face will go blue.
Dinosaurs coming
He is big and green.
Dinosaurs coming
I'm not so keen.
Dinosaurs coming
His big teeth.
Dinosaurs coming
Creeping in the leaf.

Brendon Sanger (8)
Goldsworth Primary School

1000 LITTLE LEMMINGS

1000 little lemmings walking about,
You've got to help them find their way out.

All of them there with their green hair,
What can they do while they're standing there?

You have got to knock down that wall,
Otherwise they will all fall.

Eventually they find a trap door
And they all rush out, 4 by 4.

Sammy Creasey (9)
Goldsworth Primary School

THE WEATHER

Some times in England the weather is bad,
When it's bad it's very sad.
Like when there's rain, it's such a pain,
When there's snow, I feel so low,
And when there's cloud it's dark and loud.

Sometimes in England the weather is really good,
Like when there's sun I can have fun,
When there's a rainbow I enjoy the colours of the show.

Rubiya Karim (8)
Goldsworth Primary School

MATHS

Maths is a subject which everyone likes.
We find it as easy as riding our bikes.
+ - x + are the signs that make the maths alive.
Numbers big and numbers small
Numbers large and numbers tall.
1 to 10 count again
10 to 20 that's plenty.

Abigail Lay (8)
Goldsworth Primary School

Scuba Diving

I feel alive when I dive,
I feel dead on the seabed,
I have a flare for the dare of no air.
I feel bare when I come up for air,
For there is a wonderful world down there
That I need to share.
It's rare that people take the dare
Of going down there,
But I would take the dare anywhere,
For people to share my dare.
If I had no air I would shoot a flare into the air.
So the dare would turn into air,
All because of the flare.

Adrian Roux (9)
Goldsworth Primary School

Pounds

There was a man who went into town
   and asked for a pound.
So a scoundrel gave him a pound
   and made a screeching sound,
So he chased him round town
   and bumped into a very large clown,
Who they climbed up and over,
   like a huge mound.
And flopped down, splattered all over town,
   with a huge frown.

Miles Harty (8)
Goldsworth Primary School

IN A MOMENT OF SILENCE

In a moment of silence I can hear a butterfly closing
Its calm wings
And drinking nectar from a red rose.
In a moment of silence I can hear the sun setting in
The dimming sky.
In a moment of silence I can hear a fish slipping in
the clear water.
In a moment of silence I can hear a colourful rainbow
shimmering in the soft sky.
In a moment of silence I can hear a fluffy white cloud
Floating in the blue atmosphere.
In a moment of silence I can hear a bluebell ringing its bells.
In a moment of silence I can hear a tear trickling
down a baby's face.
In a moment of silence I can hear an owl swooping
through the air.
In a moment of silence I can hear sand swirling
Round
And round
And round.

Lucy Watson (9)
Halstead School

GOD'S PERFECT WORLD OF SHAPES

The planets turn gracefully in space,
As the sun like a gold ball beams its long lasting heat on the Earth,
The moon shimmers on the oceans as night falls and looks like
a large round eye,
Circular bubbles bounce on the thin air as
Rainbow colours gleam and glow in the light,
The wind swishes round whistling as it dances in and out of the trees.

Candice Cocks (9)
Halstead School

Through That Door

Through that door
Is my secret room
Where I have a lamp
That shines in the brilliant colours of the rainbow
A beautiful carved wooden music box
That plays the songs of nature and
My four poster bed is draped with gold hangings
And my dreams are drifting thoughts in space.

Through that door
Is a magnificent garden
Where daffodils are as big as clock faces
Where the trees whisper in the breeze
Where the scent of pollen is intoxicating
And where there are many colours blushed in the sunset's cheeks.

Through that door
Is the roaring ocean
That heaves and tumbles
That rolls and sprays
That breathes steadily in and out
That laps and sucks
In the vastness of ever moving blue

Through that door
Is the city of my mind
Where dreams come true
In the moonlight.
Where troubles are forgotten and
Where I can pour my happy thoughts
Into a glistening pool of water
And see them again before my eyes.

Natasha Osborne (9)
Halstead School

THROUGH THAT DOOR...

Through that door...
Is my secret room
Where the carpet is made of cloud,
That is as fluffy as a tiger's fur.
When you tread on the carpet you sink
Into noiseless silence.
In the middle of this circular room,
You will find a sphere
If you look into it -
You will see the future.

Through that door...
Is my garden
There is a pond,
That twinkles and sparkles
In the sunlight.
Six weeping willows
Bow down to worship the tall elegant grasses.
The sun gives out gold rays.
The rockery has tiny shrubs
And huge weather-beaten rocks.

Through that door...
Is an ocean,
With white foam
Like syllabub in a bowl.
The sand is a browny bronze,
Little pebbles lie out before you and
Fish of every colour
Swim.

Stephanie Denning (9)
Halstead School

In A Moment Of Silence

In a moment of silence,
I can hear the water flow in the soft silent air.

In a moment of silence,
I can hear the blink of my eyelid.

In a moment of silence
I can hear the teardrop from my glistening eye
Trickle down my cheek.

In a moment of silence,
I can hear the golden fish slither through the blue murky waters.

In a moment of silence,
I can hear the light buzz its way through the cold gloomy night.

In a moment of silence,
I can hear the furry owl fly through the midnight sky.

In a moment of silence
I can hear the world spin in the dark space.

In a moment of silence,
I can hear the cold night air get carried away by the hot blazing sun.

In a moment of silence,
I can hear the old balloon gently lose its cold air.

In a moment of silence,
I can hear my brain thinking of what to say.

In a moment of silence,
I can hear the computer 'think' what to do,
While I direct it stressfully.

Camilla Whittington (10)
Halstead School

THROUGH THAT DOOR

Through that door,
I find a secret room,
With a magical golden book
That sings like a nightingale,
I have a mirror in my secret room,
And when I look into it,
I see all my thoughts in the mirror
Reflecting back at me and smiling too.

Through that door is the ocean,
But is not as it seems.
It is frozen,
It is like a snow world,
Held in time,
All has gone,
But in place of the fish,
Are fluffy white polar bears,
Which roll and run around on the ice,
Covered in huge baggy fleeces.

Through that door are the mountains,
Which look like up-turned ice cream cones,
Topped with vanilla sauce,
Where eagles circled round and round
Waiting to catch their prey,
And down below are the trees,
That look like chocolate flakes,
Glistening in the morning sun.

Charlotte Jackson (10)
Halstead School

THROUGH THAT DOOR

Is my secret room
Where toys come alive
And brighten up the gloom
Of a cold crisp corner of winter.
In my secret room there are
Books that take me to
Magic worlds of
Unicorns with shimmering horns.

Through that door
Is the rolling ocean
With waves crumbling on the shore
The white foam, fluffy like clouds, froths and flows.
The waves roll and twirl as if they were dancing
There the tranquil sound of whales communicating,
Graceful thoughts can be heard and
Seagulls swoop down and flap their wings like petals
Waving in the wind.

Through that door
Is the city of the mind
Where dreams disappear like butterflies
And thoughts drift into different worlds
Like clouds bumping into each other.
They are like vibrant colours
Wonderful and thrilling
And where imagination is a world of wonder
And excitement.
Through that door.

Charlie Grahame (10)
Halstead School

THROUGH THAT DOOR

Through that door is a secret room
With shining keys to a piano
Playing music,
Dreaming music,
The Magic Man plays a note and disappears.

Through that door is a black mountain.
With a dragon breathing fire
Protecting his treasure of gold.
And with shiny scales scattered
Smoothly on his body.
The mountain edges
Carved around him like a cave.

Through that door is a sea.
The sea with starfish at the top.
Waving, playing, splashing about
And his magic scales made of gold.

Through that door is a garden of ponds
With lilies protecting the water.
The shades of colour brightening it by day or night.
The birds are humming in my garden
Of ponds and colours.

Through that door is the city of the mind
With store and pets and supermarkets
Children begging their mums for every toy they see.
Parades with shining costumes
Marching on the city streets
Then it is silent
Shops close
The day goes away and the night comes in.

Elizabeth Tweedy (9)
Halstead School

THROUGH THAT DOOR

Through that tiny, red door,
Is a secret room,
There's a tree, which doesn't bear fruit
But radiant rubies and splendid sapphires that gleam and glow,
As the moonlight rests upon their smooth surfaces.
And there's an attractive rocking chair,
Where I can sit,
And think,
And dream.

Through that miniature, blue door
Is a vast ocean that flows around the scaly skin of the colourful fishes.
Where an octopus dances to the movement of the sea.
The sun rests upon the water,
Lighting the surface in sparkling threads . . .
In harmony,
In agreement,
In peace.

Through that small, purple door
Is a wonderful garden.
With a pure golden bench
And silver wind chimes
That play perfect tunes.
The grass is like a soft, velvet rug,
And the flowers never lose their colour,
And never,
Ever die.

Faye Everard (10)
Halstead School

THROUGH THAT DOOR

Through that blue door,
Is an immense ocean,
With blue dolphins
Leaping in and out
Of the sparkling waters
And creamy pearls lie
In rose pink shells,
On a soft bed of
Sand.

Through that door
Is the City of the Mind,
Where you can dream
Of wonderful things
And happy thoughts
And hopes that come true,
But nightmares are
Banished from
The City of the Mind.

Through that door
Is a beautiful garden
With pink blossom trees
And yellow daffodils
With bluebells that ring
Hyacinths that never die
And orchids that bloom
Making them look like a
Radiant rainbow
And the green grass
Lies on the ground
Like a soft velvet carpet.

Becky Rosenberg (9)
Halstead School

Through That Door

Through that door,
In my secret room,
The snowbells on the window sill ring out my happiness.
My silver stallion springs to life,
and grows to its real size.
Taking me over the moon's silent, shadowy, sphere.
In my secret room,
No worries enter,
Dream catchers don't let nightmares trouble me,
I can talk to my toys,
Laugh with the wise lunar moth.
Through that door,
I sit by the ocean, while it roars and sends the wind to fiddle
With my clothes,
Where the beautiful colour of the sea mist hides everything,
Where the seagulls float as in a dream,
And the water sparkles like a sapphire.
Through that door,
Is the city of the mind,
Where I can catch my dreams -
Be invisible,
Start a new life,
Not having to go to school,
Be famous!
But it is my world that no one can reach.

Shelley Eastwood (10)
Halstead School

THROUGH THAT DOOR...

Through that door,
Is my secret room,
Where my magnificent horse,
Comes to carry me to Mars.
When at night my puppet doll comes alive,
And plays games with my hair,
Until the sun gleams through the purple, lace curtains.

Through that door,
Are the mighty Alps,
Snowy on the top,
Like cream on meringue,
Frothy and white,
Like toffee sauce,
And shining blue rivers,
Trickle down the creamy slopes.

Through that door
Is a gorgeous garden,
With lilac lilies,
And purple pansies lying in neat rows.
There is a tall wall in this garden,
Where vines creep up every moonlit night,
Wrapping around the long bamboo stick that leans
against it.

Julia Davies (9)
Halstead School

RAMPAGING RIOT

The storm like a hippo stirs
From its sleep and he
Eyes a tasty morsel.
Slowly it moves,
Transfixed on its snack
Until it's a metre away.

He pounces and
Gnashes his teeth,
Water whirls and spits and
Drenches the prey!
The hippo roars and thrashes about
No longer quiet and still.

The African plain darkens,
As the waterhole rapidly empties.
The hippo's eyes glint maliciously and
On the stormy sky their light reflects like lightning bolts.
Drops of water are flooding the ground
And a roar of envy echoes around.

Rachel Lovibond (10)
Halstead School

THE STORM

The wind was like a person sleeping softly and quietly
Till his wife woke him up and he
Began to roar like the wind crashing together
And his wife started crying like the rain.
He stamped and shouted like the storm
And made the trees sway and fall over.

He made the seas crash and fly,
His wife cried even more and all her tears fell,
Into the rivers
And the rivers overflowed
And the storm raged.

Jane Moffat (9)
Halstead School

THE LUNDIES

As they were galloping along
The trees were falling on the ground.
Their manes were swirling around in the cold breeze like twisters.
The forelocks were moving around the eyes
As they annoyed them.
The stifles in their legs were working so hard
And sounded like thunder claps.
The storm raged again.
The horses extended into a trot.
Soon they were galloping.
The anger of the storm made the leaves come off the trees
And they were swirling around them.
They reared up into the air as the screaming wind howled around them.
Soon . . .
They calmed down to a walk.
The wind died down again
And the twister twirled into the distance.
As the sunset blushed at the end of the day . . .
Now the Lundies were walking off into the sunset.

Hazel Williams (9)
Halstead School

IF STARS WERE SEA HORSES

If stars were sea horses,
They would dance in the rock pools,
And glide through the waters.
If the moon was a glimmering jellyfish,
It would flow like a golden pearl
Through the shimmering sea,
And glint just below the surface of the water.
If clouds were sand from the bottom of the ocean,
They would float through the misty waters,
Rising in the fog,
And send showers of flowing sand instead of rain.
If planets were leaves,
They would float on top of the water,
And by the force of the gentle wind,
Would glide along the surface of the deep blue ocean.

Martha Williams (9)
Halstead School

STORM

A storm is like a person,
Like an old grandad who is struggling to get on with his life
As his long beard sweeps along the ground like a hurricane.
He blows the clouds out of his way
Not bothering about the damage he has done below.
Just caring about himself and nobody else
And he thumps his feet on the clouds and they send
Down rain to Earth
Lashing against the windows and doors
As it thumps on the ground.

Francesca Dadlani (9)
Halstead School

IN A MOMENT OF SILENCE

In a moment of silence I can hear
A shell in the sea calling me.
Calling and calling by the swish of the sea
On a wave bed.

In a moment of silence I can hear a poppy calling me
In the middle of a dew-dropped field.

In a moment of silence I can hear
An elephant from a picture calling me
Over the dry plains.

In a moment of silence I can hear
Voices of vampires calling me.
Their dirty, dusty voices call
Saying beware, beware.

In a moment of silence
I can hear a book reading to me.

Laetitia Ward (9)
Halstead School

THE STORM

The storm is like a person crying
And making the bright sun disappear
Making horrible floods so no one can go anywhere
And the sad person makes the wind turn round and round
Taking pieces from houses and swirling the leaves.
Then the person makes lightning and thundery sounds.
She stops crying
The thunder stops
And the flood gets less.

Rosie Burt (10)
Halstead School

IF STARS WERE PARROTFISH

If stars were parrotfish,
The pinpricks of light would change,
Before my very eyes into showers of rainbow sweets.
The pale, drifting jellyfish clouds
Are swallowed by the aeroplanes like shady sharks,
Who roam the dark, deathly deep.
The fisherman in the moon
Pulls in his line - the shimmering, bright tail of a comet,
And eats his magnificent catch.
The shiny planet pebbles glisten,
After the wash of the tide,
Leaving them shining like precious stones.
The night would be filled with colour,
The night would be filled with life,
Oh, just imagine if stars were parrotfish.

Joanna Ward (10)
Halstead School

THROUGH THAT DOOR - MOUNTAINS

Through that door are the mountains
I hear echoes that
Float in the soft gentle breeze
And my feet sink
In the snow,
Which is just like
A pure white layer of cotton wool
And multicoloured lights
Glint in the sunlight
And a prickly, precious pine tree is
Covered in soft snow.

Madeleine Dellner (9)
Halstead School

Storm

The willow tree slowly sways
Gently like a person singing to herself
In the afternoon sun.
Then it seems as if God has covered
His creation over
With his coat of darkness.
The clouds are dragged to the world like
Mad dogs.
Then the wind begins to blow
And the rain lashes
And the gentle willow tree seems like a
Mad woman whipping everything in her way.
The wind and the rain join together
And form patterns in the lamp posts.
The rain makes the ground soaked
And the wind pulls up the wild wet willow
And drops it in the middle of the road.
It roars!
Then God commands the wind and rain to
Stop.
All is still
And the sun comes
But the weeping willow whimpers to herself,
Asking how she was chosen to die the
Slow way!

Charlotte Worrall (9)
Halstead School

THE WIZARD

The wizard's cape flows like the river.
He's looking at what he can find for his cauldron.
Smashing
Crashing
Faster and faster as he is stirring the pot.
Like the whirlwind
Fiercer and fiercer!
Now it is working!
Raindrops fall from the sprinkle of his wand.
In comes the wizard's best friend, the lightning -
Stomping and
Crashing in the thunder's rage.
Splash!
Splash!
And a crash as the waves come in.
Finally it is calm.
The wizard's best friend has gone.
All that is left is the wizard.

Lara Redman (10)
Halstead School

THE STORM-MAKER WIZARD

The storm-maker wizard,
Whirls his cloak,
Over woods, rivers and trees,
He picks up what comes in his path,
And adds it to his bubbling cauldron the sea.
He stirs it with his magic wand,
As it thunders and roars.
It whirls round and round,
Like whirlwinds,
Crashing against shores.

The clouds stir and hiss,
The trees cry for help,
The people down below,
Try to escape.
Destruction has come,
And will not stop,
For the storm-maker wizard
Will keep it as his secret potion!

Clare Bourke (9)
Halstead School

THROUGH THAT DOOR

Through that door
There is my secret room,
With magical wonders and dreams
Toys that come to life
Sunbeams that fill the room
And there is a star which grants me wishes when I want

Through that door is my secret garden
Where daffodils glow like the sun,
Tulips come in wonderful colours
And rainbows have vibrant colours

Through that door is an ocean
Where fish dip and dive through every little particle
of sand,
Dolphins talk to each other,
Mermaids comb their hair
And watch the world go by
And angelfish swim in a heavenly water world.

Jessica Elphick (9)
Halstead School

THROUGH THAT DOOR

Through that door
Is my secret room,
Where miracles happen
Where magic lies,
Where a grand cupboard stands
In a dusty corner all alone.
As it opens
I see parrots' wings . . .
Lions' manes . . .
Tigers' coats.

Through that door
Is a garden
Full of perfumed roses,
That are as red as silky poppies
Swinging back
And forth.
Birds singing a peaceful tune sit,
Cuckoos call in amongst the blossom trees
And at night a silent owl swoops down,
Looking for a mouse in the blanket of the velvet
Midnight sky.

Dominique Dron (10)
Halstead School

IN A MOMENT OF SILENCE

In a moment of silence
I can hear the crawling of a ladybird
Searching for greenflies.

In a moment of silence
I can hear an owl silently swooping through the darkness
Searching secretly for her prey.

In a moment of silence
I can hear the ticking of a baby's brain
As it stumbles, half-walking, to its mother.

In a moment of silence
I can hear the December snow drifting
To its snowy bed
As I watch it from the window.

In a moment of silence
I can hear the hand of a watch
Walking round its face.

In a moment of silence, what can you hear?

Anna Redbond (9)
Halstead School

STORM

The clouds are crying,
Weeping because nobody likes them.
The sun is shining happily like a big friendly face,
Beaming at me.
The clouds are now getting angry,
Like a livid, fiery, furious bull.
The sun starts to feel threatened,
He hides behind the clouds.
The clouds are blowing furiously at the ground below,
Lightning is like a yellow slashed ribbon.
The clouds burst and their tears fall down,
On the people below.
The storm starts to feel tired.
Now he looks at the damage he's done.
He feels guilty,
Rivers have burst their banks,
Houses are ruined,
Then he falls asleep.
Satisfied
Content with his work.

Jennifer Douglas (9)
Halstead School

THE FLUFFY KITTEN

The wind is like a little fluffy kitten sleeping contentedly
purring silently.
Suddenly there is a bang and a crash.
It opens one eye and then the other
stretches out one paw
and starts to hiss.
It rolls over and over
faster and faster.
Tearing at the white sheet of cloud
ripping down trees
spitting at the earth.
Overflowing rivers and bursting banks.
It paws at the houses
wrecking them
tearing them to pieces
and then it takes one mighty pounce
hissing and spitting.
Suddenly
it rolls onto its back and purrs
once again.
Content.

Lucie Crawford (9)
Halstead School

THROUGH THAT DOOR

    Through that door
    There is an ocean
Where two angelfish swim in and out of each other.
As they swim to the surface,
Mermaids sit on a rock chattering,
Combing their golden hair.
A crab dances with its partner snapping at its careless claws.
An electric eel slithers along the surface of the sandy bank.
A shoal of fish swim together,
Making a shape of a diamond.

    Through that door
    Is a garden
Where flowers bloom each second all year round
And the sparrow flies in and out of the tall, mossy trees.
Tulips and roses sway in the calm breeze
And the grass is like a green velvet carpet.
The sun and the rain are welcome visitors in the garden
And there is a poppy field bursting with rich colour.

    Through that door
    Are the mountains
Where the eagle circles its nest looking for prey.
The river trickles through the mile high trees
The calm breeze blows in my face as I step on frozen leaves
And when I speak it echoes through the snow-covered mountains
Like a dying dream.

Alice Vassallo (10)
Halstead School

A BULLIED CHILD

A girl about the age of ten,
Tall and intelligent,
Bullied because she's posh and neat,
Tell-tale and crier, willing and nice.

No one wants to play with her
Because she picks her nose.
They say she has a disease as well,
That can't be cured.

We never really see her face
It's buried in her arms.
No one seems to care at all
Because of her reaction.

She never wins any race
Or competition,
Always thinking she's the best
Always being right.

I wonder what she'll be
When she grows up,
Probably an accountant
Or reporter.

But one thing for sure
She'll get further than us
Typing on her computer
Whilst we're in the dumps.

Denise Wakeford (10)
St Dunstans RC Primary School

FRIENDS

A popular boy,
Everyone likes him,
Boys, girls, everyone.
Why can't I be popular,
A sad, lonely boy like me.

Oh how nice it would be
If I could,
Just one,
Yeah one will do,
Josh has Tim,
Matthew has James,
Oh why, oh why can't I have a friend?

All the things we could do,
Climb trees, play footie
And yes we could have sleepovers.
At every one of my parties you'll be invited.

Together we'll be a community,
Something very strong.
No need to fight lions
To be a friend of mine,
You're perfect the way you are.

Craig Woodhams (10)
St Dunstans RC Primary School

THE BOY WITHOUT A FRIEND

A lonely child, no friends at all,
asking to play with someone,
but not getting an answer,
saying that it wasn't catching,
but no one ever believed it.

After a while he got fed up,
but never gave up asking.
When he asked, they just laughed and laughed,
until finally, he just gave up.

Rachel Sullivan (9)
St Dunstans RC Primary School

MY BREAK-UP

She's so boastful
Leaving me out every time
Using me to get friends.

I hate her
Acting like the queen of rights
Why do I bother?
I try to stop her from boasting.

She's so selfish
She takes everything away from me
Apart from my friendship
Where's hers?

The boys like her,
As a friend.
They used to like me.
She is so good at drawing.

I think it's just me being harsh
Or jealous.
I love her drawings
They're so neat and tidy.

Chloe Mamet (9)
St Dunstans RC Primary School

THE LONELY GIRL

It always happens to me
Oh why, oh why is it always me
She groans as she walks across the field
And yet I always think back
Somewhere in my mind I know she remembers me.

She sat alone, so alone on the wall
You know with a miserable face
Somehow crying so little I don't know how
She was such a tall girl
I thought confident, but not
So uncertain and afraid
With her sad look of misery, sat alone
Alone on the wall.

Miranda Smith (9)
St Dunstans RC Primary School

I'M MYSELF

He couldn't run as fast as people expected,
He ran as fast as he could,
But couldn't match the fastest.
People laughed as he panted in at sixth
And when he collapsed at the finish line,
But those people hadn't tried as hard as him
And when he finally did get a first place,
Those people had a go.
The person who laughed and laughed
Panted out on the fourth lap
And the others managed to match his pace
And did better,
But he didn't care for he was just himself!

Daniel Donovan (9)
St Dunstans RC Primary School

THE BULLIES

In the playground there's this boy, he bullies people,
By pushing people and calling them names.
He goes around with two other boys,
They fight with each other and get told off.
They bully anyone they fancy to bully.
It happened to me once and to my friends,
They get people into trouble.

In the classroom they play about and don't listen,
So they sometimes have to sit out in the corridor
And go to Miss Newlingward.

Rachael Jordan (9)
St Dunstans RC Primary School

T I O A F

Everyone needs a friend,
To help them,
To let their friendship bend
And stretch even further,
As far as it may go.

A friend, a six letter word.

F   riends are happy,
R   ight friendships count for right people,
I   mmortal friendships go on and on,
E   ntertain your friends,
N   ot having a friendship is wrong,
D   ots are on friendship, a special love,
S   o you see,
        T I O A F stands for,
        The importance of a friend.

Hannah-Jade Murphy (10)
St Dunstans RC Primary School

THE LEFT OUT GIRL

A girl was always left out in the playground
She was said to have germs
It wasn't very fair on her
She hadn't any friends.

How horrid they were to her
She had nothing to do
But sit and watch the others play
And have fun.

Oh how horrible she must have felt
Sitting on her own.
It must have been very sad
In the corner where she sat

She tried to amuse herself
And have fun by herself
She tried to make some friends
But they turned away.

Who would make her happy?
I would make her happy
And play with her
And my other friends

How happy she must have felt
To have some fun with other kids
Her age.

Kelly Hockley (9)
St Dunstans RC Primary School

THE MAGIC BOX

I will put in the box
A wish of a dreamer on Christmas Eve,
The dusk of December 31st,
The dawning of a new era
And all the constellations as they fall.

I will put in my box
The last drop of a melting snowman,
The teeth of a golden rabbit
And the tail of a silver horse.

I will put in my box
The sounds of a dancing wind,
A whirlwind in the purest sea
And the first cry of a baby.

My box is fashioned from
Velvet and ancient pine,
With dreams in the corners
And sweets for hinges.

I will float in my box
And twirl round in the sky.
I will land in Majorca
And run in the sand
By the sunset.

Felicity Arthur-Worsop (9)
St Dunstans RC Primary School

THE BOY WITHOUT FRIENDS

The boy without friends,
Never spoke to anyone,
Never ever had friends,
Spent playtime leaning against a wall.
At lunch he sat alone,
He was never picked for any team
And was teased all the time.
No one ever lent him anything,
Or swapped their lunch with him.
Everyone hated him and never sat next to him,
He only wore shorts and a shirt even in the winter.
His knees and elbows all scratched and cut.
I wish he could have had some friends,
If only I had been his friend.
I'm sure he would have been very happy,
If only he could have a friend,
He would not be bullied.

David Legrand (9)
St Dunstans RC Primary School

MY MAGIC BOX

I will put in my box
A slit of a scale from an ancient monster,
A crunch of ice from the Himalayas,
Ten grains of sand from the Gobi desert,
Three snips of silk from a grand sari.
I love my box and I will treasure it forever.

James Fowkes (9)
St Dunstans RC Primary School

MY MAGIC BOX

I will put in the box

A goldfish from a clear blue sea,
The stars from out of the sky
And a spell from a witch's cave.

I will put in the box

The colours of a rainbow,
A spark from the rarest ruby
And a crown all made of pure gold.

I will put in the box

A flame from the sun,
An alien from Mars
And a genie out of a golden lamp.

I will put in the box

A sunset from the end of a day,
A feather from a peacock's tail
And a first smile from a baby.

My box is fashioned

From a mixture of silver and gold,
With diamonds as the corners,
With secrets trapped inside.
The lock is the shape of a star
Falling from the sky.

I shall create magic spells in my box
And perform magic tricks,
Then fly on a magic carpet
And disembark in the land of the rising sun.

Natasia Szagun (10)
St Dunstans RC Primary School

THE MAGIC BOX

A magic box I found one day,
shining brightly in the woods,
just sitting there
still and quiet.
To my eyes it's like money
in a huge pile.

It's a gold and silver box
not like a normal box.
It's very powerful and very clever.
It can answer all your questions
and warn you of dangers.

It has a key.
I keep it in my bedroom.
It is very beautiful.

Nicola Pogorzelski (9)
St Dunstans RC Primary School

MISSILES

A missile is a bloodthirsty vulture.
As it leaps off its high mountain perch,
It soars through the air, high up
And is guided by its scattering prey.
It has eyes like scanners,
Which can be used at day or infra-red at night,
Which indicates a dive-bomb
And leaves the prey down below without a chance.
It surfaces and destroys its helpless prey
And whoever the victim, has had its last day.

Robert McClurey (10)
St Dunstans RC Primary School

THE MAGIC BOX

I will put in my box
A match played with Michael Owen,
As fast as a dragster car,
As strong as a rock.

I will put in my box
A yellow beach,
A blue ocean,
As hot as a dragon breathing fire.

I will put in my box
A red Ferrari,
An orange Liverpool shirt -
Signed by the whole team!

Steven Andrew Nolan (10)
St Dunstans RC Primary School

ALIEN SPACECRAFT

The burning spacecraft flowing through the sky,
It smells of burning as it goes by.
Coming down, coming down, landing on the ground
Crash! Crash! Crash! What a sound.
It's white, blue, pink with spots,
I see enormous blue feet with dots.
Here they come I hear squeak, squeak!
Walking out with a pointed, triangular beak.
I offer them a rosy red apple, off a tree,
They munch it and crunch it up for their tea.
Now we are friends, they are here to stay,
I hope they never, never go away.

Stephanie Colairo (10)
St Dunstans RC Primary School

THE MAGIC BOX

I will put in the box,
The whistle of an icy breeze blown on a winter's morning,
A heat ray from the gleaming sun,
A bristle from the back of a golden porcupine.

I will put in the box,
A swig from the most rapid sea in the world,
The tip of the tail of an electric eel,
The tongue of a roaring lion.

I will put in the box,
A golden wish, written in Japanese,
The last word of an ancient pharaoh,
The first sight of a baby.

My box is wooden and ancient
With iron pictures of dragons.

Gino Weller (9)
St Dunstans RC Primary School

THE MAGIC BOX

I will put in my box
the spots that come from a sprinting leopard,
hair from a lion's mane
and the swish of a tail from a cat's body.

I will put in my box
a leaf from the biggest growing tree,
the two in two thousand
and a silent wish from a glowing star.

I will put in my box
a three leaf clover from the biggest field,
all the colours from the rainbow
and the last cough from an ancient man.

Catherine Morrison (9)
St Dunstans RC Primary School

THE MAGIC BOX

I will put in the box

The whoosh of a worn wand on a winter's day,
A firefly attached to the golden fleece,
The tingle of a tongue touching a tooth.

I will put in the box

Icicles from the snow cavern,
A gulp of the clearest water from Lake Hyling,
A frog that jumped from Jamaica to Hong Kong.

I will put in the box

A fifth season and a red moon,
A sea horse in space
And an alien in the water.

My box is fashioned from fire, water and wind,
With planets on the lid and nourishment in the corners.
It's hinges are the teeth of sharks.

I shall paint my box on Picasso's easel,
Then sell my compositions
And use melted gold and silver as paint
And expensive varnish for water.

Jamie Morris (9)
St Dunstans RC Primary School

THE MAGIC BOX

I will put in my box:
The last baby born
The first cloth made
And the greenest grass.

I will put in my box:
A purple moon and a blue sun
The biggest fish
And the smallest tree.

My box is decorated with
Gold and silver
In the corners are sparkling gems
And the hinges are giants' knuckles.

I shall swim in my box
On the warm waves of the ocean blue
Then come ashore onto a snowy land
The colour of the moon.

Hannah Fidge (10)
St Dunstans RC Primary School

MY BOX

My box is fashioned from silver and iron
with sparkling diamonds encrusted
and it has a slightly blue surface.
Its hinges are made of watery white gold,
its insides are lined with furry red silk.
Inside the box is a whisper of silvery smoke
that spins into a vortex when the lid is opened.

Craig Cox (9)
St Dunstans RC Primary School

THE MAGIC BOX

I will put in the box
A drop of the finest wine,
The tooth of a dragon,
A sip of molten rock.

I will put in the box
A golden doubloon
And a touch of fairy dust,
Plus a speck of iron ore
And lots, lots, lots more.

I will put in the box
A lamp like Aladdin's,
The demon in the wrath,
A drop of water from the south
And the treasure that comes
From the cave of wonder's mouth.

Theo Jones (9)
St Dunstans RC Primary School

THE SPEED BOAT

The speed boat is a dolphin,
gliding across the water,
jumping and gleaming over the water,
for hours and hours it bobs
and when the day is dawning,
it stops and sleeps till the sun rises.

Jack Bertolone (9)
St Dunstans RC Primary School

My Magic Box

My magic box is fashioned from hard wooden pine
and the handle is a thick chunk of gold
from a pirate's box of treasure.
The box is full of dreams inside
and I shall dance in my box
and feel the sides of my shining gleaming box.

I'll put in my box, a baby's first words
and an old ancient pharaoh telling his story.
Its bolts are an overpowering bright gold
like the ray of the hot summer's sun.
The edges are a smooth silver
like the rocks on the outside of a deep,
dark mystical cave.
Inside my box there is soft red silk
like a heart that is full of secrets.

I love my box.

Victoria Valente (10)
St Dunstans RC Primary School

The Dragon

The volcano is a fire spitting dragon,
its great claws glisten in the darkness.
Sometimes he's cross and spits out fiery ashes
and sometimes he's bored and gives out a grumble
but most times he's peaceful and stands in his place
and you can barely hear a snore.

Kelly Burns (9)
St Dunstans RC Primary School

THE MAGIC BOX

I will put in the box
the first laugh of a baby,
the rainbow just after a storm,
a sunset on a sea.

I will put in the box
the look of the moon at midnight,
the look of the sun at dawn,
the look of the sun on a summer morning.

I will put in the box
a look on a child's face on Christmas Day,
the reflection of the sun on the sea.

My box is fashioned from gold and steel and stone,
with sun on the lid and planets in the corners.
Its hinges are like the gates of Heaven.

I shall ride in my box
on the cliff of Mount Everest
then land on the soft surface
of a field of grass.

Christopher Mulvihill (9)
St Dunstans RC Primary School

EVENING SUN

Dew on a spider's web
Is a snowflake in the twilight
Shining and glowing on the coastline
With jewels and stars on it
Swirling and reflecting tonight.

Kate Honeywood (9)
St Dunstans RC Primary School

MY MAGIC BOX

I will put in the box

the roar of the crowd as an England try is scored,
the powerful dark knight takes the white queen,
the swish of a golf club moving through the air.

I will put in the box

the life of an ancient mummy,
the glory of the singing birds in the morning,
the tropical fish in the gleaming waters.

I will put in the box

the happiness in people's hearts with smiling faces,
the twinkle in a diamond reflected by the sun,
the emerald shine in green shades.

My box is fashioned from the old wood
that holds a generation together
and a silk red inside.
My hinges are made of shining gold
from the crown of a lost king.
The lock is made of a hard ruby
found in the Earth's crust.

I will search in my box
to hunt for new adventures
and discover new worlds.

Ross Irving (9)
St Dunstans RC Primary School

MY MAGIC BOX

I will put in the box

A fantastic, frenzied, fabulous bear,
A gruesome grasshopper,
The fingerprint of a human.

I shall put in my box

All the power of the gods,
All the medals of the Olympic Games,
The new hair of a snowy newborn rabbit.

I will put in my box

A ginger-haired troublesome boy,
A shoelace from the 20th century,
The sphere of the global village.

My box is fashioned from

Prehistoric pine with a smooth red velvet cover inside,
A sticker of a star on the side of the box from the 24th century.

I will cycle in my box

On a great high stretch of grass,
I will have a towering purple bike
On which I will travel to distant lands.

Cathryn Samuels (9)
St Dunstans RC Primary School

TIDAL WAVE

Splashing, crashing tidal wave,
Spurting, surging, grubby caves.
Shiny, frothy, gleaming bright,
Going into the sea is just right.

Michelle Roche (10)
St Dunstans RC Primary School

FRIENDS FOREVER

Me and my friends
Have been friends forever
We are like the sunshine on
A warm day.

We play all day
And have so much fun.

But when we break-up
It is always me on my own.

All I do is stare at people
Having fun, laughing
And playing together.

I just sit and cry on my own
Until the bell goes.

Then I slowly get up
And walk in on my own.

Rachel Harrison (10)
The Hermitage School

LONELINESS

Loneliness is the worst thing.
It is like a rainy day, never-ending.
It takes a long time to get used to,
It is as upsetting as someone moving on,
You can always get lost with no friends
To help you through a maze.
People just pick on you wherever you go.
Everyone gets lonely and loses their friends.
Loneliness is the saddest thing.
Watching people playing is upsetting.
Being lonely is as boring as grass.
Walking round the playground on your own.
Loneliness is horrible.

Chris Parker (11)
The Hermitage School

YELLOW

Another day with the sun
blazing bright.
The bright sandy beach stretching
for miles.
Lightning striking fear with a
flash of light.
Lemon with a nice
fresh smell.
Yellow burning hot summer.
Yellow is like the stars
twinkling brightly in the sky.

Christopher Harper (8)
The Hermitage School

My Extraordinary Friend

She keeps me company
when I am lonely.
She cheers me up
when I am sad.
She's my extraordinary friend.

She is like a puppy
that never stops playing,
She is like a computer
that never breaks down.
She's my extraordinary friend.

We play all day together,
until the sun starts to set.
Then we head off to our beds
and look forward to the next fun-filled day.
She's my extraordinary friend.

Victoria Marshall (10)
The Hermitage School

My Dog

My dog is as stupid as a baked potato.
My dog is as sweet as a grain of sugar.
My dog is a tiger stalking its prey.
My dog runs like a cheetah.
My dog is as loud as an elephant.
My dog smells like a rose.
My dog is like a tiny ant.
My dog is mine.

Mike Slade (10)
The Hermitage School

THE ARGUMENT

There is this girl in my class,
We were as close as Siamese twins.
Until we had an argument,
Which split us right in half.

It started by her calling me an idiot,
Then I said she was as thick as a brick.
She pushed me over on the floor,
Then she disappeared out of sight.

I looked around the busy school,
I knew I had to find her
But unfortunately I had to stop,
My sad moment had begun.

I felt as though my heart had exploded into millions of pieces,
I cried like an ambling river,
I just had to go home.

I cried all night until I slept,
I felt as miserable as a tree on a deserted island.
I wanted to be friends with her so badly,
But she just backed away from me.

My eyes are filled with redness,
I look as red as the sun on a hot day.
Our friendship was so close
But now it's lost at sea.

I rang her up the next morning,
Then told her how I felt,
She said she thought the world would end,
I laughed and said so did I.

Clare Hadley (11)
The Hermitage School

BLUE

The strong blue waves crashing against the cliff or rock,

The bright blue sapphire glimmers in the sun,
The blue silent sky on a sunny day,

The flowing blue river as fast as it could be,
The smooth blue lake flowing every day,

The violets blooming in the spring sunlight,
The glinting blue raindrops falling from the sky,

The dark blue flag swinging in the breeze,
The clear blue pond as silent as can be.

Jack Pettifer (8)
The Hermitage School

WHITE

High up above, stands fluffy white clouds,
In the winter children make glaring snowmen.

People who like art use sticky white glue,
Boiling white sun can keep people warm.

If you play chess, whites always go first,
If you're good at drawing you draw on white paper.

In school the teacher writes stuff on the whiteboard,
At break time you're meant to go to the cold white loo.

Hannah Brassil (8)
The Hermitage School

WHO MADE ME?

Who made my eyes
To see and look?
Who made my ears
To listen and hear?
Who made my mouth
To eat and speak?
Who made my nose
To smell and sniff?
Who made me?

Who makes me angry
To scream and shout?
Who makes me happy
To bounce and play?
Who makes me sad
To weep and cry?
Who makes me jealous
To moan and sulk?
Please tell me who made me?

Natasha Blackledge (10)
The Hermitage School

BLUE

Blue pens working away.
Bottle-nose dolphins under blue glittery water.
Blue cars go fast always zooming past.
Class A's carpet nice and furry.
Blue tit soars through the air and finds its nest.

Michael Todd (9)
The Hermitage School

WHAT IS GREEN?

Green is the grass,
Green is a caterpillar,
Wiggling on the grass.
Green is the land,
Green is the blossom.
Green is a piece of paper.
What is green?
Green is a brush
That sways in the air.
Green is a colour of a frog
Swimming in a swamp.
Green is the colour of the pen
I am writing with.
Green is the pretty colour.
Green is a rubber.
Green is a tray.
Green is a chameleon,
Green is a cube.
Green is the green, green grass.
Green is a card.
Green is a mug.
Green is a book.
Green is a flower.
Could you imagine living without it.

Mark Boylett (7)
The Hermitage School

ANGER

Anger is a mix of things
Hatred, jealousy and cruelty.
It boils up like a kettle.
The bubbles in the water slowly rising.
Then one day you just lash out.
You cannot stop yourself.

You do so many stupid things.
You say you might even kill someone.
Anger then becomes a balloon it either floats away or explodes.
But sometimes it stays deep down inside.
Usually you say sorry and forgive.

Jeffrey Rawson (11)
The Hermitage School

BOYFRIEND MAYBE, GIRLFRIEND ALWAYS

There is this boy in class T
Who has my head all in a whirl.

But a boyfriend he probably won't be,
Because to him, I'm only a girl.
More than anything - I can't pretend.
I would really like him to be my special friend.

I think he is funny and has a lovely smile,
If I told him I loved him - he would run a mile.

He makes me go as weak as a dying flower,
But I think for now, I will stick with . . . girl power.

Did you know I have a very best friend
And I hope our friendship will never end.

She's there for me when I'm feeling down,
Or laughing at me when I am acting the clown.

We go back a long way, since we were very small
But now we have both grown up, we are in upper school.

She is a very important part of my life.

Laura Hart (11)
The Hermitage School

SPIDERMAN'S SPIDER

Spiderman's spider helps
Spiderman fights crime,

His superhero special attack
Is squirting purple slime.

He's black all over
With lots and lots of eyes,

And his super-strong legs
Can crush enemy spies.

If he falls off a building
He'll not land with a thump,

Because he'll squirt out his spider web
Which makes a bungee-jump.

He's hairy as a mammoth
With poison at the tip,

And villains beware
This spider has some grip,

And when he's rid the world
Of evil and his job is done,

He'll go home, watch TV
And have a currant bun.

Simon Jones (10)
The Hermitage School

SADNESS

Sadness is miserable sadness is upset
Sadness makes your life go dark
Sadness is rotten, badness is horrid
Sadness makes you cry and cry.

If you get beaten up you get sad
If you get told off you get sad
If you have no friends to play with you get sad
If you get called names you get sad.

John McCormick (9)
The Hermitage School

WHITE

Tap tap tap on the white computer keyboard.

While outside, coming out of white fluffy clouds
Comes white freezing snow.

I press print on the white computer,
Out comes my writing on the white flappy paper.

I now decide to play on my old chess board
With white dusty squares.

I can't play by myself so I wrap up and
Go outside to build a small white snowman.

Out here it feels like it's the South Pole
All covered in white snow.

All my white paving slabs are covered in
White wintry snow.

I look up at the roof and hanging off it
Is chilly white icicles.

I'm going shopping in my dad's
White small car.

I've learnt that white is a very cold colour,
See you soon with another colour.

Claire Couzens (8)
The Hermitage School

ZOMBIES

He is a dead man walking
He is as strong as a wrestler
He is a scary poltergeist
He is a bone cruncher
He is covered in blood like a vampire
He is as fierce as a lion
He is a horrifying creature
He is a flesh eater like a tiger
He is a cunning person
Could he be a bat fluttering around madly?
Could he be a ghost whining like a kettle?
Could he be a banshee cackling loudly?
Could he be a werewolf howling like a dog?
Could he be a phantom laughing like a mad scientist?
Could he be a skeleton rattling its bones like maracas?
Could he be a poltergeist causing havoc like a hurricane?
Could he be a vampire sucking people's blood?
Are you brave enough to enter the horrible house?

Matt Broderick (10)
The Hermitage School

REMEMBER ME

When I saw my gran my heart filled up with gold
And I think I must be bold
I know there's a part of her that's me
We both used to love to swim in the sea
Sometimes I think I see her in the cloud
But then I realise it's just a funny shaped round
I know she's gone in this life but there's a part of her in my heart
And I will see her again one day.

Phoebe Robertson (10)
The Hermitage School

Friendship

Friendship is like a bright sun shining
In a summer's day
You have someone to talk to
And someone to make you feel warm.

But when you fall out
Then clouds come rolling back
Over the sun.

When you make up
And have fun again
You know friendship has always been there.

Leanne Harrison (11)
The Hermitage School

My Puppy

It's funny
My puppy
Knows just how I feel.

When I'm happy
He's yappy
And squirms like an eel.

When I'm grumpy
He's slumpy
And stays at my heel.

It's funny
My puppy
Knows such a great deal.

Faye Elliott (10)
The Hermitage School

WHAT IS BROWN?

Brown is a tiger's stripe,
the other is black.
Brown is sometimes a butterfly,
Up high in the sky.
Brown is a tall kangaroo,
Jumping up so high.
Brown can be an eye colour,
So we can see everything.
Brown is an autumn leaf,
Drifting slowly down to the ground.
Brown is a roaring bear,
Very fierce.
Brown is a robin,
With its big red breast.
Brown is very popular
So you could not live without it.

Frances Henderson (7)
The Hermitage School

WHAT IS GREEN?

Green is a car, whizzing on the road.
Green is the grass, soft and smooth.
Green is a bush, prickly and small.
Green is paper, colourful and shiny.
Green is a tree, swaying in the wind.
Green is leaves, coming off the tree.
Green is paint, splash splosh on the paper.
Can you imagine not having it?

Scott Gill (8)
The Hermitage School

FRIENDSHIP

I broke up with my friend today,
Our time was ticking away,
Friendship can be as hurtful as
Your mum and dad splitting up,
It is like a cat and mouse
In the same room.

When they shout at you it hurts
So much, so much.
My friend went off with Robbie today,
They are so happy together
I know they don't think about me, about me.

There is a piece of my heart missing.
It must have been in our friendship together.

Thomas Eker (11)
The Hermitage School

WHAT IS PURPLE?

Purple is the flower that grows in the grass.
Purple is the paint that goes everywhere.
Purple is the paintbrush that you paint with
And the purple dress that you wear.
Purple is the rubber that rubs off
And a pencil to write with.
Purple is a pencil case that you put all your pencils in.
Purple is the lunchbox that you eat,
Everything purple is magical!

Vanessa Ma (8)
The Hermitage School

WHAT IS GOLD?

Gold is the ring
That is on my finger.
Gold is the chain
That is on my neck.
Gold is the zip
That goes up and down.
Gold is the earring
That lives in my ear.
Gold is a frame
That goes on my wall.
Gold is that paint
I love it.
Gold is the pencil case
That pencils love.
Gold is the crown
That is on the king.
Gold is the frames
That are on my glasses.
Gold is the stars
That are in the sky.
Gold is the sun
That burns your back.
Gold is the sparkle
That is in your eyes.
Gold is the popper
That pops.
Gold is the clock
That ticks.
What would we have
Without it?

Lauren Pink (9)
The Hermitage School

My Friend Lilly

I have a friend called Lilly,
That only I can see,
She's always in my bedroom,
Watching over me.

She's got brown hair and blue eyes,
Her dresses are like silk,
Although she never eats anything,
She drinks a lot of milk.

Lilly never disagrees,
With anything I say,
Unlike my sister Joanne,
Who won't even play.

One day I went on holiday,
I left Lilly behind,
She said she was so busy,
She didn't really mind.

Lilly cheers me up,
When I'm feeling sad,
But sometimes together,
We can be cheeky and bad.

When my family are too busy,
Or too tired to talk,
Lilly's there to chat to,
Or there to go for a walk.

Now I am getting older,
Lilly is fading away,
But I have lots of other friends,
Who can come round and play.

Sarah Rhodes-Brown (10)
The Hermitage School

WHAT IS GREEN?

Green is the grass
Blowing in the wind.
Green is the caterpillar
Wiggling through the grass.
Green is a crocodile
Chomping its big teeth.
Green is a feeling, flaming with envy.
Green is a chameleon
Changing colours.
Green are the sprouts
That make me feel sick.
But what will the world come to without
Green!
Green!
Green!

Steven Bartlett (9)
The Hermitage School

RAGE

I feel like I'm going to lash out
I'll take down anything I see,
I am on a mission to destroy
I want to flare out at anyone I see.

Do I fight like a ninja
Or do I just run like an antelope
Dashing from a tiger
Should I scream and shout and run all about?
Do I just sit down and stay calm?

Andrew Lawrence (10)
The Hermitage School

My Best Friend

My best friend
She always has a place in my heart
She's always there
Even if we're apart
When we fall out
It's like a storm cloud
Over my head
I'm always there
So she knows I care
When we fall out
We're hateful to each other
When we get together
The arguments are in the past
Remember friendship is a fragile thing.

Hannah Wood (11)
The Hermitage School

The Door

Go and open the door,
Maybe there's a purring cat.
The cat is brown.

Go and open the door,
Maybe there's bags of money
Falling from the sky.

Go and open the door,
Maybe there's a dog
That wants you to stroke him.

Ryan Meeks (7)
The Hermitage School

THE TRUE STORY OF ALICE IN WONDERLAND

Alice has fallen down a dark hole,
And landed in a pot of coal.
She has chased the white rabbit,
Cos she thought she could grab it.

Alice fell on a different land,
And saw the sun shining on the sand.
She saw Tweedle Dee and Tweedle Dum,
And then *bang* she saw them playing on a drum.

They said 'Please don't go, listen to us play,'
So she heard them play, and play all day.
She said 'I'm leaving,' so they smacked her on the bum,
She cried 'Man I'm getting with that Tweedle Dee and Tweedle Dum.'

She went to chase the white rabbit,
This time she did grab it.
She met some talking flowers,
They kept her singing for hours.

They called her a weed,
And she felt like a tiny bead.
She met a caterpillar called Fred,
That was eating a loaf of bread.

He said 'One mushroom will make you taller,
The other will make you smaller.'
She walked through the wood,
And bumped into Little Red Riding Hood.

She met the Cheshire cat,
While wearing a purple hat.
He said to go right,
To see a pretty sight.

She found the Mad Hatter and Hare,
She thought she was invited that's fair.
She said 'I want a cup of tea.'
Then they said 'Come on let's flee.'

Alice got mad,
They said she was bad,
So they went to find the Cheshire cat,
On the way she saw a dirty rat.

She met the red Queen,
She thought she was an angry bean,
The queen wanted to play croquet,
So Alice said 'I'll play.'

The Queen bent down and we saw her pants,
Crawling on top were lots of ants.
On her pants there were red hearts,
And she kept eating sticky jam tarts.

Will Alice ever get out
Or will she have to ride a spout?
Will she climb a wooden beam?
But, maybe it's all a dream.

Vanessa Reid (9)
The Hermitage School

ORANGE

Orange flowers on top of me
and I shine in the sea.
Little orange crabs crawl around,
there they are on the ground.

Poppy Evans (9)
The Hermitage School

CINDERELLA

Cinderella was washing the floor,
Then a shout said 'Answer the door.'
There stood a Red Setter
With a bright pink letter,
He said 'Show it to them all,
Because you're going to the ball.'
Her mother said,
'*No,* we're going instead.'
So poor Cinderella
Got locked up in the slimy cellar,
Appearing in the light
A voice said 'Are you alright?'
'I want to go to the ball
In my brand new sparkly shawl.'
'I've got a plan
So you can.'
'You may have a coach
And a huge diamond broach.'
'Be back by midnight,
Otherwise you'll have a fright.'
When she was there
She tripped on the stair.
Cinderella ate mints,
Then danced with the Prince.
Soon it struck midnight,
Cinderella had a fright.
She lost her slipper,
Because she ran quicker.
She got into the coach,
Still with her broach.
'The girl this slipper fits' the prince cried
Tomorrow she will be my bride.'
The very next morning,
(Cinderella couldn't stop yawning).

The prince travelled down,
To the awful town,
Everyone tried the slipper,
From Posh Spice to Flipper,
It was the ugly sisters' go.
The prince cried 'Help me so'
The first sister said 'It fits yippee
Now you're going to marry me'
The prince said 'Sorry my moose
It's just too loose'
The second sister tried
'Sorry my dear,' the prince replied,
Cinderella shouted 'How about me?
My gosh it fitted yippee!'

Jade Podmore (10)
The Hermitage School

WHAT IS BLUE?

Blue is the sky,
With the snowy, white clouds floating through.
Blue is my eyes,
Staring at you.
Blue is on a blue tit's head,
Sometimes it's even on mine.
Blue is the water,
Where the sun tries to shine.
Blue is sometimes a butterfly,
Flying in the sky, oh isn't it high up.
Blue is a bluebell,
And nothing like a buttercup.
But what would we do
If we didn't have any *blue!*

Alix Snell (7)
The Hermitage School

My Invisible Friend

My concealed friend is called Dino.
His favourite actor is Jean Reno.

My out of sight friend is someone who I trust.
I asked to play with him and he said 'Well, if you must.'

My disguised friend is one cool lizard.
The one thing he hates is horrible turkey gizzard.

My unseen friend is as cuddly as a furry bear.
The only problem with him though is he doesn't seem to care.

My unperceivable friend's favourite film is *Jurassic Park*. Whenever he thinks about it he's pleased his ancient ancestors left a mark.

My indiscernible friend has a heart of solid gold.
He had a house of toy boxes but now it's sold.

I share a special friendship with my inconspicuous friend.
But sometimes he gets on my nerves and drives me round the bend!

Paul Martin (10)
The Hermitage School

The Tree

Sighs when the blustery wind blows its leafy hair,
Its hair rustles in the wind crunching its branches,
Grumpy when it's windy, happy either rain or shine,
Its hair rustles and its leaves fall off to blanket its feet.
Never shows its arms when a man is near,
Its eyes are brown and when it has a date it puts green gel on its hair,
Its roots are its legs where it has a quick drink.
With its hands it gives us oxygen to breathe in.

Thomas Smith (9)
The Hermitage School

MY COUSIN AND HER BEST FRIEND

My cousin and her best friend
Break up every week
They always include their friends in it
Every time they speak.

Like a fragile petal falling off a flower.

We really get fed up with it
We wish they'd stop some day
We never get to play a game
Only if they're away.

Like a fragile petal falling off a flower.

They argue over the strangest things
Like a silly little pen
Then after a few days
They are friends again.

Like a fragile petal falling off a flower.

Eleanor Beamish (11)
The Hermitage School

WHAT IS GREEN?

Green is the grass, sparkling in the morning dew,
Green are the trees, waving in the sunny breeze,
Green are the bushes, sprouting flowers over spring,
Green are sour limes, ripe and ready to eat,
Green is the sea, glinting over into the horizon,
Green is the sign of life, movement and nature.
Green, when we think of it, makes us think of jealousy.
Green means calm and quiet.

Michael Veale (8)
The Hermitage School

BEING PICKED ON

I was the small one always around
I was the one that you called names
The one that didn't look happy
I was like a bug getting trodden on

I never went away
I was always at your side
I was never as happy as you
But now you've gone

I was wrong you weren't nice
But I have moved on
And got lots of friends
I'm as happy as a hyena

Now my life is a lot better.

Stephanie Sale (10)
The Hermitage School

SPACE

Roaring rockets zooming
White moon destroying
Orange sun self-destructing
Huge satellite beeping
Red Mars whizzing
Small shooting stars gleaming
Fascinating asteroids darting
Satisfying Saturn soaring.

Robert Scott (11)
The Hermitage School

Best Friends

Our friendship is as
fragile as china,
It takes up a part of our heart.
It is as warm as the sun scorching down on us
and we are always there for each other.
We are as strong as a piece of metal
and as hard as a rock.
Breaking-up would be like a storm cloud over your head.
But we would never break-up.
We both make each other laugh like hyenas.

We will never break-up.

Shakira Westbrooke (11)
The Hermitage School

The Unicorn

The unicorn is a marvellous mystical creature,
She moves gracefully not making one sound,
Like a ballerina dancing across the stage,
Her silver coat stands out like white against black.
Her wonderful horn is opalescent,
Shimmering like a fresh pearl,
Newly pulled out of the sea,
She has the most beautiful tail made out of silken strands,
Her mane is a plait of silver and gold thread.

Briony Chamberlain (10)
The Hermitage School

WHAT IS WHITE?

White is a blossom
Hanging on a tree.

White is the part
You can't remember in a dream.

White is a yacht,
Sailing in the breeze.

White is mucky
Slushy yucky paint.

White is snow,
Falling softly on the ground.

You may not notice,
But white is all around.

Sara Dunford (8)
The Hermitage School

WHAT IS BLUE?

Blue is the sky,
The air is blue.
Blue is a pair of shoes.
Blue is a boat sailing on the blue blue sea.
Blue is a jumper that people wear.
Blue can be a chameleon that turns blue.
Blue is a shirt that people get.
Blue is a canoe sailing on the lake.
What can we do with blue?

Adam Charman (7)
The Hermitage School

WHAT IS BLACK?

Black is the black night
when all the glowing stars come out.

Black is a cute guinea pig
running up and down.

Black is a dangerous puma
in a deadly jungle.

Black is a wild rabbit jumping up and down.
Black is some ink dribbling down a pen.
Black is a fierce meat-eating bear.
Black is a fluffy coat.
But black might be boring,
But the world is a much better place with it.

James O'Daly (8)
The Hermitage School

WHAT IS ORANGE?

Orange is a ball,
Floating to the shore.
Orange is an orange
That is sweet.
Orange is a T-shirt,
That you wear.
Orange is a book,
That you read.
Orange is a paint
That you paint with.
Orange is a tiger flaming hot.
Orange is a piece of paper nice and strong.
Orange is my favourite colour.

Aaron Broderick (8)
The Hermitage School

FOOTBALL CRAZY

Football is a good game,
It's fast, keeps you fit,
Supporters sing and chant their team name,
Some may stand and some may sit.
It's played with a round ball,
Eleven or seven players are on each side,
The aim is to score a goal,
And not kick it wide.
My favourite team is Chelsea,
At present they are on the up,
And if they beat Arsenal on Sunday,
They'll probably win the cup.

Mikey Burningham (9)
The Hermitage School

THE DOOR

Go open the door
Maybe there's a ghost
In the haunted house creeping about.

Go open the door
Maybe there's a monster
Scaring everybody out of their pants.

Go open the door
Maybe there's a huge spider
Spinning its web.

At least it scared you.

Jack Slater (8)
The Hermitage School

BLUE

Dangerous daring considerable blue sea.
Wet wonderful swimming pool.
Sloppery slippery ice cube nice and cool.
Cold lips gone quite blue.
Gleaming blue eyes looking around.
The enormous blue sky lovely and blue
Facing the ground and looking at me and you.
Happy glad children going to school
Looking smart in their school uniform.
The teachers wearing a cotton dark blue sweater.
Heavy large bags being hung up.
Beautiful soft petalled bluebells.
I end this poem and I'm going home
In my zooming blue car.

Lisa Russell (9)
The Hermitage School

ON A SPOOKY NIGHT

Last night someone came to our house
He was so quiet he was silent as a mouse
He crept into the kitchen to help himself to some food
When I had found that out I thought it was rather rude.

That night I couldn't sleep
So I tried counting fluffy sheep
I went downstairs and dropped all my bears.

I went to the kitchen holding a wooden bat
Just then I found out the stranger was a cat.

Lauren Buffone (10)
The Hermitage School

The Door

Go and open the door
Maybe there is a secret garden
With animals you have never seen before.

Go and open the door
There might be trees
Or a place that is always sunny.

Go and open the door
Maybe there's kind people who never fight
At least it won't be scary.

Jessica Lawrence (7)
The Hermitage School

The Door

Go and open the door,
Maybe outside there's
A spiky dinosaur roaring.

Go and open the door,
Maybe outside there's
A palace full of gold
And dancing people.

Go and open the door
Maybe outside there's
A garden full of wonders.

At least we'd be rich.

Rachel Thornber (9)
The Hermitage School

WHAT IS BLACK?

Black is the night where stars shine so bright,
What is red?
Red is roses growing over the fences.
What is blue?
Blue is the sky shining all around us.
What is yellow?
Yellow is the stars sparkling in the sky.
What is green?
Green is the grass glistening on the ground.
What is white?
White is fluffy white clouds floating along.
I love every colour in the world
But my best are blue and red.

Amy Potts (7)
The Hermitage School

NIGHT

Have you ever stayed awake at night
It's really scary then.
It's the time when werewolves howl
And all the trees go rustle
No one's there to help you then
But what's that tapping on the door?
Is it a witch or a banshee?
I'm really scared so go away,
I think I'll go to sleep.

Robbie J Ashton (9)
The Hermitage School

WHAT IS COLOURFUL?

What is red?
Red is a heart pumping up and down.
What is green?
Green is a camouflage colour that blends in with the ground.
What is red?
Red is as beautiful as love.
What is green?
Green is a bush that rattles all day.
What is red?
Red is a person's hair on fire.
What is green?
Green is leaves falling off the trees.
Green and red are my colourful colours.

Rikkie Letch (8)
The Hermitage School

MONSTER

It is gooey ooey and its name is Looey,
It is elastic as flubber,
And it stretches like rubber.
Teeth like knives which scares all the wives,
Everywhere it's green even its spleen.
It's fat as a rat which scares all the cats.
It's rough and tough as a bone which can karate chop a stone.
It's cold as ice which freeze the mice.
It's very slimy and this poem is rhymy.
It's a monster and it's got hands like a lobster.

Robert Estcourt (10)
The Hermitage School

COLOURS

What is black?
A silky cat prowling down the street.

What is red?
A poppy's red shining in the sunlight.

What is green?
The grass is green swaying in the wind.

What is yellow?
The sun is yellow glistening over the world.

What is white?
The clouds are white moving every day.

What is blue?
The sea is blue crashing at the rocks.

Jack Sollis (8)
The Hermitage School

ANGRY THOUGHTS

In my mind I do feel
Cross or am I hurt?
Do I cry or do I fight?
Do I burn or do I fall?
Do I swear or do I shout?
Why do I shout and shout?
Because I am like a screeching car
Do I feel terror or do I feel weak?
No one knows that except me.

Yashar Baghri (10)
The Hermitage School

WHAT IS BLACK?

What is black?
The night is black
Filled with starry stars
Formal wear is black
Riding in flash cars.

Red is like
A red red rose
On the wall
With its greatest pose.

What is blue?
The sky is blue
Filled with white clouds
Blue is the sea
That is so very loud

What is green?
The grass is green
Like an evergreen tree
The stem of a flower is green
Attracting every bee.

What is yellow?
The sun is yellow
Giving off hot heatwaves
An oil lamp is yellow
Travelling through every cave

Colours colours
What will we do without
Colours?

Conor Carr (9)
The Hermitage School

My New Friend

'We broke up today,' moaned Sarah Brown,
I knew our time was ticking away,
Since the competition,
It was ticking ticking ticking away.
Since the competition,
She went off with Ricky,
It's like a part of me is missing,
Since the competition,
I thought she would come back,
But she never did,
It's five weeks now,
Since the competition,
I've got a new friend now,
She's called Cindy Loo,
We play together, laugh together,
But we'll never get split up by a silly competition,
For she is imaginary.

Alana Francis (11)
The Hermitage School

What Is Multicoloured?

White is the colour of a snowman
Black is a storm with a strike of light
Blue is the colour of the sky
Yellow is the colour of a hot sun
Orange is the colour of an orange
White and black are the colours of a penguin
Red is the colour of a
Valentine's heart
Silver is my favourite colour to beat!

Juliana Mills (8)
The Hermitage School

ANIMALS

Animals are all different things in the end
Because hamsters are soft, cuddly and sweet.
Kittens are joyful, playful and active.
Giraffes are long-necked, thin and yellow.
Lions are fierce, mean and scary.
Mice are small, tiny and squeaky.
Leopards are enormous cats, spotted and not striped.
Elephants are huge fat and big eared.
Cheetahs are fast and they run like the wind.
Tortoises are slow, have a hard shell and live in dry places.
Monkeys are loud, furry and flexible.
Rabbits are cute and their tails are fluffy.
Foxes are a reddy colour, aggressive and have long bushy tails.
Snakes are vicious, scaly and have poisoned fangs.
If God made animals and humans all the same
The world would be a boring sight.
That's why everyone and everything is different.

Lauren Reynolds (10)
The Hermitage School

BLACK IS . . .

Black is like a rhino galloping through the field
Black is a jumper itching for its freedom
Black is dull but very useful
Black is a beetle staggering down the street
Black is steaming out of a train
Black is a woodpecker gnawing in a tree
Black is the best!

Jack Warren (8)
The Hermitage School

WHAT IS BLUE?

Blue is the sky
As the clouds go by
Blue is the jumper on our uniform
Blue is the water in the sea
Blue is where you want to be

Blue is the colour
On your cap
Blue is the sea
On your car map
Blue is where you want to be

Blue is a bird
In the tropics
It's in the jungle the animals heard
Blue is as cold as an iceberg
And blue is where you want to be.

Becky Partridge (9)
The Hermitage School

WHAT IS WHITE?

White is snow that falls from the sky,
White is a snowman wearing a tie,
White is something that shows up on black.
Why?
White is the colour of the clouds way up high,
White is the colour of cotton wool
All wrapped up in a ball
But best of all I like white.

Kate Greentree (7)
The Hermitage School

Gold

Gold is for jewellery and art,
Gold is for flowers,
Splitting apart gold is for
Highlights and scarves.
Gold is lightning and grease.
Gold is for twinkling suns
And gritty sand and stars
And don't forget summer's here again.
The light twinkles so bright,
In the shining sunlight.
The light of cars shine in the
Dark and misty nights.
Gold can be colours of walls
And duvets.
Gold is a warm and cosy colour.

Rebecca Thornber (9)
The Hermitage School

Bluebells Blue

The sky is blue
It looks like it's covered in blue glue
Everything is blue, except for you
Blueberry ripple, blue feathers that tickle
Velvet hats can be blue
But not as soft as blue cats
Blue can be lipsticks but not for dipsticks.

Rachel Tooley (8)
The Hermitage School

THE BREAK-UP

I had a break-up today.
Me and Jane Smith.
There was pinching, hitting,
Screaming, kicking, yelling,
Name calling and hatred.
She went away with Mary.
I was left to play on my own.

I have a new best friend now.
She's called Sarah Petenon.
We play together, laugh together,
Joke together, sing together,
Run together and work together,
Jane asked to be my friend again,
I said no, not after the way she treated me.
I'll never break up with my friend Sarah.

Anna O'Dell (10)
The Hermitage School

WHAT IS A COLOUR?

Red is the bricks in a grand hotel
Red is the fire in a small motel
What is black?
The roof is black
On top there is a small black cat
Red is the colour of the hearts
Red is the feathers on the darts.

Daniel Oliver (8)
The Hermitage School

FRIENDSHIP

Friends are as cheeky as chimps
Or as bad as a baboon
Friends are just the same as everybody
Some are kind and nice
Some are as bad as bullies
But the best friends of all are the same as you
They don't have to be as vicious as a guard dog
Or as nice as a poodle
They're in the middle so they can be
As dumb as a tortoise
Or as clever as a teacher
Or as fast as a pig
Or as soft as the beautiful wind
They're the best of all.

Alexander Ward (10)
The Hermitage School

SPACE

The eye-catching plants float,
The entrancing universe gravitates
Mystical ventures rotate
The silent Milky Way orbits
Breathtaking zodiac gleams
The blaring comets plummet
Frigid space is moving
The mesmerising rockets zoom
The ochre planets spin
Tiny aliens twisting
Nippy mercury swirling
The speedy space spins.

Emma Wakefield (11)
The Hermitage School

NEW FRIEND

I have lots of friends,
Mark, John, Paul and Tom
But one of them is moving
I think I just might cry
His best friend only talks to me
But even to me he's shy.
To me he's my best friend now
And I'm his best friend too
Without me he'd do something stupid
Like kill a dog 'Bow, wow.'
The name of my best friend now
Is the great Liam Francis
He took me to Disneyland
But saw something and stares
You might have guessed, it was a friend
It was Thomas Claydon
He ran over these very fast
Without help from his maiden.

Oliver Grant (9)
The Hermitage School

SPACE

The burning stars shimmer
The roaring rockets blast
The ochre aliens staring
Deafening spaceships plunge
Mystical dust orbits
Eye-catching nebula glistening
The silent universe floats
The brown dust descends
As the shiny sun rotates.

Daisy Hulke (11)
The Hermitage School

FRIENDS

I broke up with my friends today.
So I played Dungeons with Hannah and Jade.
They got fed up because I was cheating.
Then I saw Charlie and Faye playing with Nick and Tom.
And then they called me along.
Nick pushed Charlie so she went in the medical room.
And Faye went to play with Hannah and Jade.
I saw Jess alone, I felt sorry for her so I played with her.
We asked Justin, Davies and Eker to play Dungeons with us
They said 'Yes.'
When we started playing Charlie came out of the medical room
And asked if she could play with us.
We said 'Yes.'
Faye, Jade, Hannah came and asked if they could play.
We said 'Yes'
The boy said they need more boys so they went to get Nick and Tom.
We all played Dungeons together and we all said
'No more breaking up!'

Rosie Hart (9)
The Hermitage School

MY BEST FRIEND

My best friend is as kind as a kitten
My best friend is as joyful as a chimp.
My best friend is as funny as a puppy
My best friend is as confident as an actor.

My best friend can swim very well
My best friend can run very fast
My best friend is very kind.
But best of all he's my best friend.

Lee Massey (9)
The Hermitage School

WHAT IS BLUE?

What is blue?
Blue is the sky where white swans can fly.
What is green?
Green is the leaves swaying above your head.
What is pink?
Pink is beauty, pale and bright.
What is black?
Black is as black as an old top hat.
What is yellow?
A sunflower is yellow with soft petals.
What is multicolour?
Multicolour is everything!

Emily Lacy (8)
The Hermitage School

I LIKE THIS GIRL

I like this girl,
She doesn't like me,
She plays with all my friends,
She doesn't play with me.

I like this girl,
She doesn't like me,
I stare and look all day,
She just looks away.

I like this girl,
She doesn't like me,
I ask if I could play,
She just says 'Go away!'

Ellie Date (10)
The Hermitage School

NE BODY

When I was a bit smaller
I had an extraordinary friend -
the fact no one else could see him
drove me round the bend.

He was as small as a mouse,
as light as a feather -
he wore a biker's jacket
made out of magic leather.

He had trousers to match it
they were black and long
he worked out at a gym
so he was really strong.

He was as strong as an angry giant,
as fast as a cheetah chasing its prey,
as clever as a fox
on hunting day.

But he's not around any more
he disappeared one day
he said he'd gone for good now
and wherever he was he's going to stay.

Michael Bird (11)
The Hermitage School

THE DOOR

Go and open the door.
Maybe there's a
bag of gold glittering
in the moonlight.

Go and open the door.
Maybe there's a
dragon breathing fire.

Go and open the door.
Maybe there's a
castle with tall towers.

Go and open the door
even if there's only
a knight.

Aaron Gauntlett (7)
The Hermitage School

RED

Red is a radish
As crunchy as can be.
Red is a rose petal
As smooth as silk.
Blood is red spitting
Out every ten seconds.
Rubber rings are red,
Searching in the pool,
But red is a heart
Beating really fast.
A Liverpool shirt
Racing round the field,
The players thinking we won!
Red is a Ferrari
Racing round with
Its engine roaring
And racing round the track
But red is danger
You're haunted all about.

Nathaniel Vries (9)
The Hermitage School

BEING LONELY

I am as lonely as a sea-washed rock
Sad as a lost child
I don't want to be lonely any more
I want to have friends and play.

I need people to talk to.
But children ignore me
Unhappy as a stray bear cub in the forest.
I want to have friends and play.

I am left out of games like a cactus standing in the desert.
Tears stream down my eyes.
I want to have friends and play.

Dani Simancas (11)
The Hermitage School

THE TEDDY BEAR

Look in its eyes, you'll have a chat
You'll talk about this and that.

Cuddle it at night
You won't get a fright.

Hold its hands
They don't feel like elastic bands.

Love it
To bits.

It'll tell you it cares
All this from teddy bears.

Laura Quinn (11)
The Hermitage School

WHAT IS BLACK?

Black is a storm with a strike of light,
It zigzags down with all its might,
Black is lots of beautiful clothes,
Hanging down in the window.
Black is bats, dull wild animals,
They like to eat bananas and apples.
Black clouds - black bats - black clothes
Black!
Black is as dark as a tunnel.
Trains going through as fast as they could,
Black is a haunted house, dark and scary,
Ghosts coming to get you very rarely.
Black is always dusty,
It makes your room all dirty,
Black tunnel - black storm - black clothes
Black!

Peter John Morgan (7)
The Hermitage School

BLACK

Black is midnight, shining and dark,
Black is coal, burning on the fire,
Black is creepy, like a haunted house,
And as scary as the Devil.
Black is a storm, with thunder and lightning.
Black is mean, mean enough to shake a boulder.
Black is the witch's cat, evil and sly,
Black is the beetle crawling along.
Black is useful, is it not?

Ben Lawn (9)
The Hermitage School

BATH TIME

When my mum says it's time for a bath
I can't wait to get in.
The bubble bath smells like lemons
So I put a lot in.
My bath is hot but not too cold,
I like it nice and deep.
When the bath is ready and full
I jump, skip and leap
And then when the bath is finished
And all the bubbles have popped
I feel so very, very sad
As I wish it would never stop.
The soft, fluffy snow coloured towel
Is wrapped around my skin
I feel so clean and warm inside,
I know I'm as clean as a pin.

Matthew O'Daly (11)
The Hermitage School

WHAT IS COLOUR?

As red as the rose I give to you.
Blue is the sea that we swim in at summer.
Green leaves swaying on the trees.
As yellow as the tall sunflower with its smiling face.
As white as a cloud in the sky.
Black as a penguin.
Orange as the sunset at the end of the day.

Rachel Wheeler (9)
The Hermitage School

My Favourite Colours

What is red?
Red is a red, red rose in a gigantic field.
What is yellow?
Yellow is as yellow as the sun in the desert.
What is green?
Green is when the leaves fall down off the trees.
What is white?
White is a swan swimming in the shimmering lake.
What is orange?
Why an orange is just an orange.
What is a rainbow?
Why a rainbow is just a rainbow.
Multicoloured is the best!

Jack Reynolds (8)
The Hermitage School

Colours

Red are the roses on the garden wall,
Yellow are the dresses of ladies at a ball.
Pink is a pig in its mud bath
Green is a child skating down the path.
Blue is the sky as the sparkling stars go by.
Orange is a sunset setting in the sky.
Black is a storm when the branches sway.
White is the snow on a winter's day.
Brown is a dog going for a walk.
Peach is the people having a talk.
These are the colours you never forget.

Leah Bannister (9)
The Hermitage School

Multicoloured

What is red?
My heart is red
What is blue?
The sky is blue
What is pink?
A flower's pink.
What is green?
The grass is green
What is yellow?
The sun is yellow
What is purple?
A juicy plum
What is grey?
A velvet shoelace
What is shiny silver?
The King's throne
What is beautiful gold?
A mirror that shines upon you.

Shauna Fox (8)
The Hermitage School

Yellow

Yellow reminds me of
The silk petals of a daffodil
and the lovely heat of the sun.
A yellow car is zooming by
Yellow reminds me of
The sandy beach
and the Liverpool shirt.

Luke Nye (8)
The Hermitage School

BEST FRIENDS!

My best friend is very special
She is always telling jokes
We play together every day
She is as lively as a tiger.

My best friend is tall and pretty
She likes drawing, like me
We both love chocolate!
She is as bright as a yellow sun.

My best friend and I argue sometimes
She shouts at me and I yell at her
We always make up though
She can be as noisy as a lion.

My best friend and I are alike
She likes pizza and so do I
We are like two peas in a pod
She is my best friend ever.

Amy Dillon (10)
The Hermitage School

FEELING

When you're happy, you're like the sun
When you're sad, you're like the rain
When you're angry, you're like thunder
When you're sulking you're like a cloud
When you want revenge, you're like lightning
When you're jealous, you're like the wind.
But when you're dreaming, all you are is you!

Ella Walding (10)
The Hermitage School

ORANGE

Flaming orange flickers like the shimmering sun,
Slimy orange octopus slithering around the deep sea,
Diving orange hats swimming around the deep pool,
Dry orange sand glinting in the bright sun,
Inky orange pens smudging onto rough paper,
Fluffy orange wool making lots of different shapes,
Shimmering orange bonfires gleaming in the moonlight.

Catherine Taylor (9)
The Hermitage School

SPACE

S pace is like looking under your duvet late at night,
P ut your thumb up to the window,
A nd you can see the moon is just a speck,
C rash, bang, whoosh, as a rocket goes up,
E lectrics fly up into the air as a rocket goes down.

Faye Groves (11)
The Hermitage School

ORANGE

Orange is the colour of the wallpaper on your wall,
Red and yellow make orange, a lovely colour.
Orange makes a rainbow,
Orange is dawn in April,
Orange is what makes a brick.
Orange is the hot sun
Burning its rays.

Megan Riley (7)
The Hermitage School

THAT FEELING

You think of a feeling for a moment.
After a moment you speak and you still get that feeling.
After a while you think that you can never get rid of it.
It's always in the back of your mind, thumping away.
When you're asleep it goes for a moment.
When you wake up it comes back.
You can never get rid of that feeling.

Ellen Potts (9)
The Hermitage School

BLUE

Blue is the colour of the sea waving on the beach,
Blue paper rattling in the wind,
Flames are blue trying to keep you warm,
The blue paint running down the smooth wall.

Hannah James (7)
The Hermitage School

YELLOW

Yellow is the bright sunshine.
Yellow is a beautiful sunflower.
Yellow is a speeding car.
Yellow is a strip in a rainbow.
Yellow is a sign of happiness when we say hello.
Yellow is the Teletubby, Laa Laa.

Georgia Smith (7)
The Hermitage School

I HATE POEMS

I've never been good at poems,
Because I can never think what to write,
I would rather do something boring,
Like running or flying a kite.

I hate poems,
I'd do anything to get away
From writing poems
At school every day.

Although I hate most poems,
There is one that beats the rest,
Not metaphors or similes,
It's limericks that are the best!

Dan Hart (10)
The Hermitage School

THE DOOR

Go and open the door
Maybe there are bright-eyed
children talking.

Go and open the door
Maybe there're teachers
drinking and talking.

Go and open the door
Maybe there's a big playground
with boys playing football.

Go and open the door
At least teachers are
on playground duty.

Katie Mynard (9)
The Hermitage School

Yellow

The yellow gleaming sun is scorching upon us,
Lovely sweet yellow lemons good to eat,
Bright daffodils, lovely and soft with yellow petals,
Yellow bananas, bright and good,
Yellow sweet corn you eat it in your dinner,
Yellow sand you find it on the beach,
Yellow sticky honey, it's very nice to eat,
Annoying yellow parrots squawking all day,
A torch that's yellow is very bright.

Hannah Knox (7)
The Hermitage School

The Door

Go and open the door.
Maybe there's a land of money
some chocolate, some real.

Go and open the door.
Maybe there's a place called Springfield
where everything is a comedy.

Go and open the door.
Maybe there's a waterfall
glittering in the sun.

At least you have all
the fun in the world.

Matthew Beamish (9)
The Hermitage School

CASTLE

Big and tall with bloody walls,
A moat that looks like a swimming pool,
A drawbridge opens,
With a squeak,
Through the horses and knights come through.

Up the stairs, climb and climb,
Near the top there's a mop,
For sweeping all the stairs,
There's a table called Paul,
Everyone eats on him
And they don't leave anything,
At all.

Hayley Chappell (10)
The Hermitage School

BLUE

Water we drink to keep us alive,
You get it in your eyes when you cry,
School jumpers and pencils,
Paper and sky,
You find it at the beach,
A hat and a bag,
Violets and doorbells
And football clothes.
Ribbons in your hair,
Glasses on your eyes,
Blue is all around us,
Just look and see.

Luca Naclerio (8)
The Hermitage School

My Favourite Friend

My favourite friend, we play games all day and we have lots of fun.
If I need someone to talk to, I would talk to him, we have tons of fun.
If we broke friends, it would be like the world breaking in half.
My favourite friend is always there when I need him and I am
There for him if he needs me.
My favourite will help me out if ever I am stuck and
I would help my friend out if he was out of luck.
It's nice to have a favourite when I am feeling low,
He is always there and makes me care about
Other people too.

Henry Deacon (10)
The Hermitage School

The Door

Go and open the door.
Maybe there's
a classroom
full of smart, educated children.

Go and open the door.
Maybe there's
a land of money,
sprinkling down coins.

Go and open the door.
Maybe there's
a beach with people
playing in the sea.

At least you will get wet.

Daniel Marshall (8)
The Hermitage School

When I'm Alone I Feel...

I feel as lonely as a tree,
In the middle of a meadow,
I feel like screaming because
I'm so bored,
I feel as lonely as . . .

I feel as lonely as a toy,
Sitting on a shelf, the last one.
I was a punch bag because
I was lonely.
I feel as lonely as . . .

I feel as lonely as a single
Bee buzzing through the air.
I feel like a single seed,
Growing up alone.

I feel as lonely as . . .

Grace Millican (10)
The Hermitage School

I Went To School Tomorrow

I went to school tomorrow,
I sat at the front seat at the back,
The teacher gave me some paper to work
I gave it her back nice and clean.
I paid for a bus and walked it,
So school was fun tomorrow.

Jade McGill (10)
The Hermitage School

LITTLE RED RIDING HOOD AND SNOW WHITE

There was once a wolf called Morph,
Who hated the seven dwafts,
He came up with a plot,
To poison the lot
And that was his mission henceforth.

Alas alas the dastardly deed,
Unfortunately did not manage to succeed,
For his eyes were playing tricks,
So he could only count to six,
So he ran off into the woods at great speed.

The one that got away was Dopey,
As he was in the bath getting all soapy,
Snow White and Red Hood arrived at the wood,
To find the dwarfs poisoned. They stood
And hung their heads feeling very mopey.

But they were quite unaware,
Of the wolf's evil glare,
As they entered the house,
Morph crept up and pounced just like a mouse.

But just as he did,
The tin bath slid,
He was launched in the air, off he went flying
And poor little wolfy was very loudly crying
Dopey had hid.

But now he came in with only a towel on his head
The wolf thinking he was dead
Suddenly fled!

Lotty Eker (9)
The Hermitage School

YOU FORGOT ME

I am as lonely as a rock at the bottom of the sea,
I'm still around under the stairs,
Kicking about our ball
You forgot me!
Once you set a place for me
Up at the dinner table
And then I was as happy
As a clown being clapped
And cheered with flowers flying all around,
You forgot me
Oh please
Oh please
Come back to me
I'll be as happy as a
Fish swimming in the sea
Oh please, oh please come back to me,
So we can slide down the banister,
Go and catch a bee, oh please
Come back to me you totally and
Utterly forgot me,
We'll chase the birds and fire peas,
Oh please, oh please you forgot me,
So please, oh please come back to me,
I'll be as happy as can be.

Alex Davison (10)
The Hermitage School

FEAR

When you fear something it takes over your mind,
It's like a bomb shattering your brain,
When your mind has a fear of something you avoid it
And don't stand up to your fears.

When you break up with your friends you avoid
Them because of the fears they might cause you.
Everyone has at least one fear in their lives,
Everyone has fears.

Bradley McManus (10)
The Hermitage School

YELLOW

Yellow tulips, light and tall,
Yellow thunder thumping the world around,
Yellow Smarties yummy to eat,
Yellow baskets being cluttered about,
The yellow sun shines above us,
Little fish yellow and shiny,
The yellow amazing stars in the sky glimmer all the time,
Bright yellow wrapping paper ready for someone to open.

Melissa Jones (7)
The Hermitage School

SUNLIGHT

When you close your eyes at night,
You wake up and you're in the daylight,
Pain shoots into your eyes,
Just like the sun staring at you.
Hotter and hotter I've had enough
And I jump out of bed and
I feel really rough.

Josh Preece (10)
The Hermitage School

BLUE

A suffering melting blue ice cube
Sitting on a boiling table,
A world covering sapphire blue sky
Just sitting there at the time.
Smacking splashing blue waves
Hitting the sand,
Frozen blue lips shimmering in the
Freezing cold,
Shiny blue water sparkling in the sunlight,
Smashing blue school uniform and
The latest fashion too,
Zooming blue cars going along the road,
Tidy blue sea with dolphins in it.

Stephanie Gale (8)
The Hermitage School

THE DOOR

Go and open the door,
Maybe there's a beautiful girl
And an ugly beast.

Go and open the door,
Maybe there's a fairy godmother,
With her godchild Cinderella.

Go and open the door
Maybe there's a spinning wheel
Where Sleeping Beauty gets pricked.

Go and open the door,
At least there'll be a fairy tale.

Natalie Howard (9)
The Hermitage School

INDESCRIBABLE FRIENDSHIP

I broke up with my friend, on a matter
I cannot describe,
We had been friends for a long time,
Always playing and laughing,
Until we let problems evolve.
Separating was the biggest step of all steps.
I felt like a part of me had been torn out forever.
The coldness ran over me.
I just could not bear the thought of being alone,
No one to help me with problems, no one to talk to.
So we forgave each other for all the problems
Between us and started a new beginning,
Just me and my friend.

James Gale (11)
The Hermitage School

WHEN I MET MY BEST FRIEND!

Before I met my best friend,
I didn't know anyone.
I was really scared to go to school
In the beginning.
When we had to go out for play
I didn't have any friends,
There were lots of children playing together.
Then this girl came up to me,
She was as shy as a mouse, she said
'Would you like to play with me?'
And I said 'Yes.'
I was as happy as a dolphin diving.
At last I have a best friend just like everyone else.

Jessica Green (10)
The Hermitage School

RED

Red is the sign of love,
Red makes me remember Valentine lips so sweet,
Roses beautiful and proud,
Red is mean, red is nice,
Red is blood when you cut yourself,
Red is brave, fierce, but calm,
Red can burn and make
A spot on your nose,
Red makes you feel warm and cosy,
Red is a fire engine going nee naa,
Red is the best!

Laura Atkinson (8)
The Hermitage School

THE DOOR

Go and open the door,
Maybe there's a
Beanstalk
Ready to be climbed.

Go and open the door
Maybe there's a
Girl dancing with the prince.

Go and open the door
Maybe there's a
House topped
With sweets
Waiting to be eaten.

At least there'll be
A fairy tale ready to be read.

Leila Prescott (9)
The Hermitage School

Friends

Friends can be like the weather
Sometimes good,
Sometimes bad,
Friends are like a two way road,
Because you both have to like each other.
Friends should trust each other even if it hurts.
Your family are your friends as well because
You can trust them
And they care for you.
Most of the time is great,
Especially if you spend it with a mate,
Friends, friends,
Friends are kind.

Rebecca Prior (10)
The Hermitage School

Yellow

Yellow fish swimming
Around in the tank trying
To say 'hi'.

Glittering stars go passing by.

Yellow hair sways in
The beautiful air.

Yellow sand sinks in
The rocky ground.

Yellow daffodils sway
In the gentle breeze.

Gemma Collyer (8)
The Hermitage School

Red

Red is the colour
Of sweet teddy bears.
Red is a loud fire engine
And a noisy one too.
Red is a chair that
Creaks and creaks.
Red is a heart
What beats away.
Silk paper is red
And that's just
Like my button.
Red is the blaze
Of a warm cosy fire.
Red is my bed,
Goodnight.

Stephanie Snook (7)
The Hermitage School

Friendship

Friendship is so delicate
You can't live without it,
Even if you want to.

Friendship is worth a million pounds
When someone shows how much they care,
Show them how much you care.

Friendship is like
Two turtle doves,
Caring for each other.

Friendship is so important and
When two people care for each other
Friendship's in the air.

Julia Roffey (10)
The Hermitage School

ORANGE

Orange reminds me of
Autumn leaves gently blowing
Off the trees.
Orange is the busy
Bees that make their
Beehives in trees.
Orange is the lovely
Flowers, they grow upon
April showers.
Orange is a baby's mittens.
Orange is building bricks
But no use to orange clips,
An orange football moves
About, it won't stop
If you shout.
Orange means fun, fun, fun!

Bryony Rose Lambert (7)
The Hermitage School

RED

Red is for Ferrari
And the race goes on.
The fire engine is red
And puts out hot fires.
Roses are red
And are love on Valentines.
Red is a heart
That beats all day long.
The sun is red
And very hot.
Red is a T-shirt
And a very hot collar.
The pictures are red
And very good.
Red is fire
And very, very warm.

Stephen Sweetland (8)
The Hermitage School

THE DOOR

Go and open the door
Maybe there's a
Land of chocolate or a
Land of everlasting sweeties.

Go and open the door
Maybe there's a
Magic beanstalk with huge
Ugly giants or kind rich people.

Go and open the door
Maybe there's snow
Covering the ground
Or a land of wishes.

Go and open the door
At least there'll be happiness.

Jessie Hart (8)
The Hermitage School

GOLD

Gold is a princess
Pretty and kind,
Marriage and love,
Seems a sign of gold.
Angels are gold,
Gold is silent, happy and
Joyful, so beautiful
And bright is gold.
It shines like the sun
Down on the Earth.
Golden rays pour down
On the ground.
A rainbow has not got gold
But gold is a lovely colour.
Golden gold, golden gold.

Emma Clarke (7)
The Hermitage School

FRIENDSHIP

I've got a best friend
At my school,
She's kind and caring for me.
She's always there when I need her most,
She's the best friend there
Could ever be.

We have our bad days,
We have our bad fights,
Friendship is something that grows deep inside.

It's not an easy thing to get
If you have friendship
Don't let it go,
Friendship is like a river that flows.

Kellie Le Marquand (9)
The Hermitage School

THE DOOR

Go and open the door
Maybe there's
A candy land
With green chocolate.

Go and open the door
Maybe there's
A jungle with
Spiders and snakes.

Go and open the door
Maybe there's
A mud factory
With mud squirting
Out the top.

At least you can
Get something to eat.

Jack Eker (8)
The Hermitage School

YELLOW

Yellow is when
Lightning comes shouting down,
Yellow reminds me of
Nice warm coats.
Yellow reminds me of
Bananas and lemons to eat.
Yellow reminds me of
Shorts and T-shirts.
Yellow is when I'm on the beach,
Yellow is when I'm in my swimming costume.
Yellow reminds me of straw
That's on the farm,
Yellow is when I'm happy.
Yellow is like a picture of art.

Rachel Gill (9)
The Hermitage School

GREEN

Green is the colour of the scary jungle.
Green is the colour of the bouncy frog.
Green is the colour of the tip of a tree.
Green is the colour of the country breeze.

Green is the colour of tasty lettuce.
Green is the colour of nasty sprouts.
Green is the colour of a soggy lily pad.
Green is the colour of a prickly Christmas tree.

Green is the colour of the summer leaves.
Green is the colour of a bright flower stem.
Green is the colour of a fully grown tree.

Daniel Fisher (8)
The Hermitage School

GREEN

Green is all around you
Green as the grass you walk on.
Green is on a tree,
Green is sloppy paint
That sticks on the walls.
Green is an eye that
Stares at you,
Like a swimming turtle that
Is in the sea.
Green is like a snake
That slithers away.

Lydia Day (7)
The Hermitage School